CARLTON FREDERICKS, PH.D.

Dr. Fredericks is a noted nutritionist and food researcher, and during 1975–76 he was the president of the International Academy of Preventive Medicine. In this new book, his emphasis is on the *kind* of calories and carbohydrates you consume, and on helping you to avoid "foodless foods." If you follow Dr. Fredericks' advice, you will eat the calorie companions your body chemistry needs for improved health—and at the same time diet away the extra fat your body doesn't need and you don't want.

Books by Carlton Fredericks

Carlton Fredericks' Calorie and Carbohydrate Guide
Carlton Fredericks' High-Fiber Way to Total Health

Published by POCKET BOOKS

Carlton Fredericks' Calorie and Carbohydrate Guide

by Carlton Fredericks

PUBLISHED BY POCKET BOOKS NEW YORK

CARLTON FREDERICKS' CALORIE AND
CARBOHYDRATE GUIDE

POCKET BOOK edition published January, 1977

This original POCKET BOOK edition is printed from brand-new
plates made from newly set, clear, easy-to-read type.
POCKET BOOK editions are published by
POCKET BOOKS,
a division of Simon & Schuster, Inc.,
A GULF+WESTERN COMPANY
630 Fifth Avenue,
New York, N.Y. 10020.
Trademarks registered in the United States
and other countries.

ISBN: 0-671-80824-9.

Printed in the U.S.A.

Contents

Why You Need This Book

Whether your fat imprisons you, or you're merely concerned with a few surplus pounds, or you're a fortunate soul who merely wants to avoid gaining those excess pounds, this book will help you take the first important step toward a slim, buoyant, youthful you.

You're not alone in seeking to achieve or maintain normal weight. About seventy-nine million adults—nearly half the population of the United States—are overweight. And if you're not one of those then you're probably among the ten million currently on or intermittently faced with the need to go on a reducing diet. That's why our country has a ten-billion-dollar fat-fighting industry. That's why we have a network of health spas and reducing salons that gross nearly a quarter of a billion dollars yearly. Users of diet pills spend about fifty-four million dollars on the pills every year, and about one billion dollars is spent yearly in the diet food market.

Your concern with your weight is understandable. Fat is more than unsightly. Excess weight, even a small amount, is a burden. Have you ever tried carrying a ten-pound package around all day? It makes your heart work harder. It puts a strain on your circulation. It helps to bring on diabetes, and worse. Your social life is affected by excess weight, and so is your job. And as for the enjoyment of life in general, no one who is fat can honestly subscribe to the "fat but jolly" mis-concept.

Why are so many Americans fat—and getting fatter? Though you know the penalties for extra pounds, you still gain weight, or have to fight not to gain it. Why? For the majority, the answer is too many calories—you simply eat too much, not only for your height and (normal) weight, but in terms of your physical activity —or, more often, your lack of it. And you eat too much out of habit, or because eating is a way of reliev-ing nervous tension, or because you fail to realize the high calorie values of your meals and snacks.

Since most people with weight problems are bur-dened by consuming too many calories, eating less food —and emphasizing low-calorie foods—is obviously the sure, effective way to lose weight or to avoid gaining weight.

For others, a minority of weight-gainers, the answer is not found in counting calories from all foods, but only in counting those taken from the *wrong* foods. Starches and sugars create special problems for these special people, and for them, cutting carbohydrates (starches and sugars) is the most effective way to achieve and maintain normal weight.

For a still smaller group—small in percentage of the population, but very large in terms of excess weight —the answer is partially found in a quirk of body chemistry. Unless a physician can find a way to straighten *that* out, such people can lose weight only by cutting down on food very drastically—far more than an average overweight person must.

No matter what type you are, the ultimate answer to the problems of weight gain and normal weight maintenance lies in knowing the calorie values of foods, as well as in knowing whether starches and sugars are your enemy—and, if so, in knowing the carbohydrate values of foods.

This book lists not only the number of calories in foods, but carbohydrate counts as well. It thereby fills the direct needs of a majority of people concerned with excess weight. You'll notice that I've given you metric values, too, so that when the United States changes to that system, your calories and carbohydrates counter will continue to be useful to you.

Let's backtrack, now, and take a closer look at calories. You can't see them until they surface on your midriff, but they're real. Food supplies energy, and the calorie is the way of measuring that energy. Foods high in calories supply much energy; those that are low in calories supply little. Our bodies need energy, even when we're sitting or sleeping and the need rises, of course, when we're physically active. If we eat enough food to supply the calories needed to play a game of tennis or to run a marathon and we don't spend those calories, the body converts them into fat. Textbooks give us the picture, in almost the same words: "If your diet supplies more calories than your body uses, you'll store the surplus energy values as fat."

One pound of fat is equal to 3,500 calories. Add this number of calories to those you need to sustain your daily energy requirements, and you'll gain a pound; subtract it, and you'll lose a pound.

It sounds easy to stay within the bounds this arithmetic dictates. Simply spend as much energy (as many calories) daily as you take in, and your weight will stay unchanged. Take in more calories than you spend, and you'll gain; fewer, and you'll lose. It seems so simple—so why are so many people concerned with extra pounds?

For one thing, people often don't know the calorie values of foods. They say: "I hardly eat a thing—I eat like a bird!" It is tempting to say "Yes—like a vulture!" And you are driven to reminding such people that birds eat an astonishing amount of food. Their calorie requirements are very high—flying is an energy-burner. For a person who doesn't fly like a bird, eating like one piles up calories the body can't burn and will inevitably store as fat.

Most people don't realize, for example, that ordinary applesauce provides about 115 calories per portion—it's high in calories because so much added sugar is used by the cook or manufacturer. Unsweetened applesauce—which *is* available commercially—has only 50 calories in a portion of the same size. The difference doesn't sound world-shaking, but fifty extra calories per meal, when they're not needed, add up to 27,000 in six months—and that translates into about eight pounds of fat stored at your middle, on your thighs, on your bottom, on your upper arms. Moreover, should you be the type of person who gains weight most readily by eating excess starch and sugar, the sweetened applesauce will not only prod your body into storing fat but will encourage you to store fluid as well, creating a double problem.

Fatty foods particularly deceive those who have not learned to be calorie-watchers. The calorie value of starches and sugars is four to the gram—roughly 120 to the ounce. Protein foods—eggs, cheese, fish, and meat—also provide four calories to the gram. But such foods supply fat, too, and fat has *nine* calories to the gram. Thus, the fats in meat, eggs, cheese, and similar foods—which we think of as "good," high in protein—constitute a calorie trap for the unwary. The butter and margarine you use in frying, or spread on bread, are similar calorie traps, for they, too, are high in fats.

Form the habit of checking your meals and snacks against your calorie and carbohydrate counter. You may well discover that some of your selections are unnecessarily high in calories—and that there are alternate choices that will help you to achieve and maintain the weight (and the figure) you want. You will probably also discover that you're eating much more than you thought—and much more than you can possibly burn up as energy.

The best way to discover what you're doing is to note what you eat. Keep a diary for a few days—and don't cheat! Make a list of everything you eat or drink, both at meals and as snacks, and then use your calorie and carbohydrate counter to total your calorie intake.

Consult the table on pages 42-43 to approximate your calorie need. If you are taking in significantly more than you require, you have a simple, quick answer to your problem: Don't feed your body furnace more fuel than it can burn. Unlike the furnace in a house, the oversupplied one of the body manages to store excess fuel. As fat. And for most people, simple calorie restriction is an effective way to weight control.

At this point, some readers will say: "For the great majority of people, yes—but what about those who seem to put on ounces when they *smell* a cake baking? And what about those who can *eat* the whole cake with no problem?"

Given that such a person has no underactive thyroid to blame (about which more later), what becomes of the arithmetic of calories in such a case? For such cases do exist. And why have doctors and nutritionists remained blind for so long to the fact of such cases? Isn't it true that the doctor to whom such remarks are addressed frequently accuses his patient of cheating, of eating more calories than he or she is willing to admit?

The fact is that there is a minority of calorie-counters

for whom the *source* of the calories is just as critical as their number.

Not too much is known about differences in man's nutritional needs and tolerances though we do understand a great deal about such variations in pigs, steers, horses, and pedigreed dogs. Unlike humans, they have a cash value, so they are carefully checked. But all we know about humans is that man's nutrient requirements vary from individual to individual, and by very large factors—exactly as they do in animals.

One person may maintain nitrogen balance with as little as two ounces daily of meat, fish, fowl, cheese, or other protein. On the other hand, there are those who require more than ten ounces of the very same foods to achieve exactly the same equilibrium. Requirements for amino acids, the building blocks of proteins, are neatly fixed by authorities—but in real life, the needs of humans have been shown to vary greatly from one individual to another, differing sometimes by a factor of more than five. Vitamin C requirements in animals may differ by a factor of *thirty*—and there's evidence to show that man's need for this vitamin is no more uniform.

Nonetheless, we create a mythical "standard reference American" with *average* requirements for protein, calcium, amino acids, Vitamin C, all other nutrients, *and calories*. It all fits neatly into computer programs, but it doesn't always jibe with the reality of variations in human nutritional needs.

There are many ongoing investgiations into the range of human requirements for nutrients, but none that I know of is concerned with calorie needs. Yet there *are* cake smellers who gain weight, and cake eaters who don't. For these people, the carbohydrates (starches and sugars) may be the mischief-makers.

Some physicians may be skeptical about reducers

who vow that they are sticking to their restricted diets and yet are not losing weight, but it's a fact that there *are* people who don't lose weight with simple calorie-restriction regimes, *unless* they also change the proportion of carbohydrates to proteins and fats in their diets! Translation: They lose if the reducing diet is low in starches and sugars; they don't if it isn't—even when the *calorie* values of the two diets are identical.

To understand this, you must drop your concept of "normal" when it comes to modern man's present choices of foods. What we eat today is wildly different from what we ate during our evolutionary years. For millions of years, man secured the energy to meet the challenges of a hostile environment from his ordinary daily diet—which didn't contain the bread, sugar, cereals, and other carbohydrates that now constitute the sources of 50 percent of our calories.

Man could not have bread until agriculture was invented, flour mills constructed and baking techniques developed. Wheat, rye, barley, buckwheat, corn, and oats were originally grasses, grown by Nature first and then by man, and used originally to feed cattle. High-starch foods could not have been in man's menus much before twenty-five thousand years ago. Sugar wasn't introduced, in its concentrated form, until about 900 B.C.

Shifting to such foods was a drastic change in the habits of a primitive creature who was a hunter and a herdsman, and not originally a farmer nor accustomed to the foods made available by farming. Nature never supplied starches and sugars in concentrated form. Man accomplished that and then tried to adapt himself to a type of menu—high in carbohydrates—with which he had no physiological experience.

Adaptation to such foods is neither quick nor automatic. Neither is it universal, as any diabetic, hypoglycemic, or patient with elevated triglyceride levels can readily testify. But there is a type of nonadapter to our high carbohydrate diet who, unfortunately, is still struggling for recognition. This is the individual who finds it difficult to avoid weight gain even when consuming the "correct" number of calories derived from a "balanced" diet.

For such a person, starches and sugars often become addictive, and the craving for them obsessive. But that is only part of the difficulty. When such individuals go on an orthodox reducing diet—which restricts calorie intake but continues to derive 50 percent of them from carbohydrates—their bodies become:

1. Overefficient in the conversion of carbohydrates into fat
2. Retentive of salt
3. Retentive of water, based on salt retention

Reducing is essentially a process of oxidizing (burning) fat, and one of the combustion products is water. If carbohydrates make you retain salt, and thereby force you to retain water, your weight will not change significantly—you will merely have substituted water for fat in your tissues. Some physicians deal with water retention by restricting salt intake and administering diuretics (drugs that promote excretion of water). This approach, obviously, represents treatment of the symptoms rather than the cause.

The proper approach to such a problem is neither diuretic drugs nor salt restriction, but reduction of carbohydrate intake. The calorie value of the reducing diet for the "carbohydrate addict" may be the same as that of any standard weight-loss diet, but the number of calories supplied by sugars and starches is cut down, and the number supplied by proteins and fats is raised. On such a diet, "carbohydrate addicts" often reduce successfully, particularly if part of their fat is taken from vegetable oils.

For those who don't respond to ordinary reducing diets, and for whom the low-carbohydrate diet is also ineffective, failure to lose weight can sometimes be traced to underactivity of the thyroid gland. Disturbances of this thermostat of the body will alter energy needs, sometimes minimizing them so much that normal food intake will result in weight gain, and a reducing diet will fail even when such a diet is so restricted in calories that it verges on starvation. This is why tests of thyroid function are routine in the practices of physicians specializing in the treatment of obesity. Although the thyroid is often unfairly blamed for the results of surreptitious trips to the refrigerator there are times when the gland *is* misbehaving and is very much a part of the overweight person's problem.

Thyroid trouble is not always recognized as such because the test for thyroid function may be misleading. For example, when the thyroid test pronounces the gland to be "low normal," it offers the possibility that "low normal" for *you* isn't really normal, but underactive. Physicians will sometimes cross-check the results of such an equivocal test by asking you to take your underarm temperature when you awaken in the morning. If it is below 97.8 degrees Fahrenheit, they will treat you for underactivity of the thyroid, regardless of other test results. (The temperature test is sometimes surprisingly accurate as an index to the need for thyroid supplementation.)

Treatment for an underactive thyroid can enable you to escape from starvation diets and still lose weight. This treatment can also bring relief from such thyroid-related problems as colds, poor growth of nails and hair, constipation, and fatigue.

None of this negates the importance of calorie-counting, for it isn't underactivity of the thyroid gland by itself that makes people gain weight. It is the *combination* of excessive calorie intake and an underactive thyroid that causes trouble.

An intriguing variable affecting weight control, and yet having little relationship to calorie intake, is the *timing of meals*. Six small meals daily in place of the usual three larger ones will usually make weight maintenance or weight loss easier. This device (which is effective in both laboratory rats and man!) also makes it easier for the body to control the metabolism of starches and sugars—not only in reducers, but in diabetics, hypoglycemics, and those who must constantly resist a tendency to gain weight. Explanations for the phenomenon are theoretical. It has been conjectured that small meals are not as well utilized as larger ones, since they do not elicit as sharp a rise in the output of digestive enzymes. At any rate, frequent eating yields better results for calorie-counters than infrequent, larger meals.

The healthy person with "average" biochemical responses safely uses appetite to govern body weight. But that automatic regulation doesn't run smoothly for an entire lifespan. In many people it works beautifully for the first forty years—despite an intake of tons of foods and liquids, it manages to stabilize weight within a pound or two. But in the early forties and the fifties, many people find that while appetite is following the lifetime pattern, the weight responses are not. Food habits often don't change, but metabolism does. The amount of physical activity often changes, too, and compensation—either in your menus or through deliberate physical activity appropriate to your individual needs and tolerances—becomes essential. Frequently a combination of both may be necessary if the thickening midriff of the forties is not to be followed by the fatness of the fifties.

One of the mischief-makers in this period is the cocktail at lunch or before or after dinner. Alcohol yields almost as many calories as sugar and starches, and, in a number of ways, fits itself into the chemistries of muscular work and the production of body heat. Furthermore, partial replacement of carbohydrate or fat in the human diet by an equal amount of alcohol has been effective in the synthesis of body tissue. But the capacity of the body for oxidizing alcohol is limited; if you take in more alcohol than your body can burn up, a chain of unpleasant consequences follows.

Here, too, there are variables. A person on a high-carbohydrate diet, particularly if it is high in sugar, will be less tolerant of alcohol than those on other types of diets. The calories in alcohol are real, and when alcohol is taken with sugar—which is so frequently an ingredient in beverages and cocktails—it becomes a formidable contributor to weight problems. Exercise won't compensate, either. The physical effort needed to work off a few cocktails is discouragingly great.

Alcohol brings us to the subject of foods containing "empty calories." By this I mean foods that offer nothing but energy (calories) while causing fatigue and doing other damage because they lack body-building nutrients.

The relationship between food energy and food nutrients is more fixed than most people realize. It requires half a milligram of thiamin (Vitamin B_1) to oxidize a thousand calories of carbohydrate. Given regular doses of calories from sugars and starches—minus the vitamin—the body is faced with an impossible demand.

This is somewhat analogous to trying to run an automobile engine without sparkplugs.

In the body, the result of taking in calories but not having the "spark plugs" is a kind of smoky half burning of said calories. Intermediate products, many of them toxic, accumulate when calories are not thoroughly burned. That's why the addition of substantial amounts of sugar to a diet in which there is a marginal supply of Vitamin B_1 results in symptoms indistinguishable from those of severe neurosis. Such a diet may produce unpleasant results ranging from hypochondria to insomnia (and bad dreams when sleep is achieved), from shortening of the memory and concentration spans to maniacal outbreaks of rage.

One miracle of life is the body's ability to burn foods at a temperature of about 98.6 degrees. If you don't think that's miraculous, consider that you can't burn sugar in a match flame until you dip the lump of sugar in cigarette ashes, which act as a wick. The "wick" in the body is a group of nutrients—the B vitamins (particularly thiamin, riboflavin, and niacin), metals such as zinc, and numerous other food factors required to maintain production of indispensable enzymes.

A second miracle of life is our ability not only to use food as a source of energy, but also to incorporate it into the structure of the body itself.

Neither of these miraculous things can be done with calories alone, and that is why "empty calories" or "foodless foods" are so sinful. Offering the body fuel it cannot utilize for energy or for repair of its structure is obviously foolhardy.

Deficiencies in specific nutrients the body metabolism requires virtually never create the desire to eat. The effect on the body is the opposite—hunger is turned off. It as though the wisdom of the body recognized the futility of fuel that confounds its chemistries. Deficiency in *calories*, on the other hand, is the key to unleashing the drive to eat—but a distinction must be made between "hunger" and "appetite." It is hunger that calls for a meal. It is appetite—the memory of pleasant experiences of the palate—that lets you eat apple pie à la mode, containing eighteen teaspoonfuls of sugar (empty calories) per portion, after hunger has been well and truly satisfied by a steak and a salad.

The company your calories keep is as important to you as your supply of food energy. Generally speaking, when you consume "whole" foods, you take in both the calorie and all its important nutritional companions. Knowing this should lead you to avoid sugar, and steer you toward organ meats, as well as steaks, chops, and roasts. It should also motivate you to buy whole-wheat bread in place of white; it should persuade you that an egg, however much it has been maligned, must be the most complete of foods—which it is. You should proceed to eat the beet tops as well as the beets. Your rice should be whole—which means brown; your cornmeal should not be degerminated, your barley should not be pearled, and you should choose whole rye in crackers and bread. Present calories to your body chemistry as they should be presented—with the nutrients that guide the calories to their appointed pathways in your organism.

There are several things that influence your success in coping with calories. We have carefully measured the calories a human needs to climb stairs, sit still, jog—but there are people who trot upstairs and those who plod; there are fast and slow joggers; there are those who slump into chairs and those who perch on the edge, as if ready to leap up. Calorie needs in persons performing the "same" activity will obviously not be the same, though body weights may be. Energy-spenders exist—so do energy-conservers. Consider how *you* do things when you're figuring out how many calories a day *you* need.

Success in controlling your calories will be greater if you not only familiarize yourself with the calorie values of common foods as you find them in this book, but also take advantage of nutritional labeling on canned and other foods. When you realize that one serving of pineapple has 140 calories and about the same nutritional value as the strawberries that are low both in calories *and* carbohydrates, you take the first step toward a pattern of food selection (and rejection) that will shape your diet *and* your body. If you compare the assays of tomato juice with those of apple or pineapple juice, you'll begin to set up a system of choices that ultimately will operate by reflex, without your even thinking about it. One look at the calorie value of a hamburger, with its usual high fat content, as compared with the fat and calorie values of broiled halibut or any other white-fleshed fish, and you'll make automatic choices. So keep notes of what you consume, consult this book regularly, and total your calories as well as your carbohydrate intake.

Since many people feel conspicuous referring to a calorie or carbohydrate chart in a restaurant, here is the full outline of a reducing diet that you can follow when you're away from home—without taking out your calorie and carbohydrate counter. Because this diet specifies actual size of portion, the calories are counted for you—all you have to do is keep an eye on the size of those portions. I call this system "dieting without drooping."

Dieting Without Drooping

This system creates no deficiency—except in calories. The diet is balanced in protein intake and contains enough fat and carbohydrate to keep body function unimpaired.

In this diet, every effort has been made to keep vitamin-mineral intake as high as possible. However, a diet below 2,400 calories is very likely to be deficient in vitamins and minerals; that is a risk inherent in reducing the gross intake of food. It is recommended, therefore, that you supplement this diet with multiple vitamins and minerals in capsules. These will not interfere with reduction, but will help to avoid deficiencies of the type that have made reduction hazardous in the past.

By the code system employed, and the lists of foods, the need for set menus is eliminated. Thousands of overweight persons have followed this diet safely—without weakness, deficiency, or hunger.

Menu for Breakfast
one serving of fruit
one egg or egg substitute
half a slice (thin) whole-wheat toast with half a level teaspoonful butter

one glass of skimmed milk
one cup of coffee or tea (optional);
no sugar, cream, or milk

Menu for Lunch

one helping of lean meat, fish, fowl, or meat substitute
one vegetable from vegetable list A
one salad (from salad list)
one serving of fruit or dessert
one glass of skimmed milk or buttermilk
one cup of coffee or tea (optional);
   no sugar, cream, or milk

Menu for Dinner

one cup of soup (optional)
one helping of lean meat, fish, fowl, or meat substitute
two vegetables from vegetable list A *plus* one from
   vegetable list B

or

one vegetable from vegetable list A *plus* one from
   vegetable list B *plus* one helping of salad (from
   salad list)
one portion of fruit or dessert
coffee or tea; no sugar, cream, or milk

Choose foods from the following lists:

Desserts

fruit cocktail (with fruits from fruit list); small
   portion
cantaloupe cocktail
orangeade (with one and a half oranges, half
   a lemon, an egg white, and saccharine for
   sweetening)
whole gelatin with fruit (from fruit list)

Eggs and Egg Substitutes

plain omelet
poached egg
soft-boiled egg
hard-boiled egg
raw egg
cottage cheese (four tablespoons)
lamb chop (one small, lean)
lamb kidney (one)
calf's liver (two ounces)
mutton chop (one small, lean)
buttermilk (one glass)
skimmed milk (one glass)

Fish

sea bass (¼ pound)
bluefish (¼ pound)
cod, fresh or salt (¼ pound to ½ pound)
flounder (¼ pound to ½ pound)
haddock (¼ pound to ½ pound)
halibut (¼ pound)
kingfish (¼ pound)
pike (¼ pound)
porgy (¼ pound)
red snapper (¼ pound)
scallops (⅔ cup, raw measurement)
shrimp (⅔ cup)
smelt (¼ pound)
weakfish (¼ pound)
clams, round (ten to twelve)
crab meat (one crab or ¾ cup flakes)
lobster (half a small lobster or one cup flakes)
mussels (four large or eight small)
oysters (twelve large)

Fruits

orange (small)
grapefruit (half, medium size)
apple (small)
pineapple (two average slices)
peach (one)
cantaloupe (half, medium size)
melon (two-inch section of average size
    melon)
tangerine (large)
berries (½ cup)
apricots (two, medium size)
grapes (twelve)
cherries (ten)
pear (medium size)
plums (two)
nectarines (three)
persimmon (half, small)
fruit juices:
    grapefruit, orange (unsweetened; six
    ounces)

Meats

lean beefsteak (¼ pound, about one inch
    thick, 2½ inches square)
roast beef (two slices, about three inches
    square, ¼ inch thick)
beef liver (one slice, three inches square,
    ½ inch thick)
beef tongue (two average slices)
beef kidney (¼ pound)
hamburger (¼ pound)
calf's liver (¼ pound)

lamb kidneys (two, average size)
lamb chop (one, about two inches square,
    ½ inch thick)
roast lamb (one slice, 3½ inches square,
    ¼ inch thick)
mutton chops (two, medium size)
boiled mutton (one slice, four inches square,
    ½ inch thick)
roast veal (one slice, three inches by two
    inches, ¼ inch thick)
veal cutlet (one, average size)
veal kidneys (two, average size)
chicken, white meat (two slices, four inches
    square, cut very thin)
chicken, broiler (half, medium size)
chicken gizzards (two, average size)
chicken livers (two, medium size)

Meat Substitutes

cottage cheese (⅔ cup)
eggs—poached or omelet (two eggs)
buttermilk (two cups)
whole milk (one cup)
skimmed milk (two cups)

Salads

tossed greens
watercress and lettuce
radish and watercress
celery and cabbage
pimento and greens
baked stuffed tomato (with cottage cheese
    and chopped celery)

One teaspoonful of salad dressing may be used. Divide between lunch and dinner, if salads are eaten twice daily; use vinegar or lemon juice to augment.

Soups

consomme
clear vegetable soup
beef broth
chicken or mutton broth
other clear soups

Note: No creamed soups or soups containing milk, vegetables, meat, or cereals are allowed.

Vegetable List "A"

asparagus (fresh or canned; eight)
string beans (½ cup)
wax beans (½ cup)
beet greens (two heaping tablespoons)
broccoli (one five-inch stalk)
brussels sprouts (½ cup)
cabbage, cooked (½ cup)
cabbage, raw (¾ cup, shredded)
cauliflower (½ cup)
celery (five stalks)
chard (½ cup)
chicory (½ cup)
eggplant (½ cup)
endive (ten medium stalks)
green pepper (one, medium size)
kohlrabi (two heaping tablespoons)
leeks, chopped (⅓ cup)
lettuce (ten leaves)

radishes (five, medium size)
sauerkraut (½ cup)
spinach (½ cup)
tomatoes, fresh (one)
tomatoes, canned (½ cup)
tomato juice (½ cup)
watercress (ten pieces)

Vegetable List "B"

beets (two heaping tablespoons)
carrots (two heaping tablespoons)
chives (six)
dandelion greens (three heaping table-
     spoons)
kale (two heaping tablespoons)
onion (one small)

parsnips (two heaping tablespoons)
peas (two heaping tablespoons)
pumpkin (three heaping tablespoons)
rutabaga (two heaping tablespoons)
squash (two heaping tablespoons)
turnips (two heaping tablespoons)

Special Notes

Sugar substitute—Use saccharine sparingly if you must
have beverages sweetened.

Water consumption—No more than four glasses daily
for first four days; then as much as you please—
provided that you do not drink more than one glass
of water at meal time.

Extra butter allowance—At lunch *or* dinner, one level
teaspoonful of butter may be used on your vegetables. If you prefer, you may use a teaspoonful of

salad oil as a dressing on salad (at lunch *or* dinner —not both). If you use the salad oil it replaces the butter. Lemon juice may be substituted for salad dressing if you elect to use your fat allowance as butter on your vegetables.

Appetite cheaters—If your appetite is hearty and dieting is annoying because of hunger pangs, do the following:

1. Avoid soups—they are optional anyway and they tend to stimulate appetite.

2. Drink a glass of cold water (within the limits allowed by the diet) when appetite presses you.

3. Use protein tablets between meals—they check appetite.

4. Choose a salad instead of one vegetable at meals.

Supplementing this diet with bran has proved very helpful to those reducers who can resist anything but temptation. Bran provides bulk, which helps to minimize the tendency to constipation some people encounter when they reduce their gross intake of food; and bulk is often very effective in creating a sense of satiety, which helps to reinforce your will power—or, more pertinently, your "won't" power.

A bran supplement can also be used if you're following a low-carbohydrate reducing diet (see page 30). While bran does contain carbohydrate, much of it is present as fiber—which by definition is not available to the body—and the requisite dose of bran by weight is small, for it is a light substance. With the low-carbohydrate diet, the bran serves the same useful purposes it does in the ordinary low-calorie diet: it provides bulk for normal elimination and helps bolster your feeling of satisfaction at the end of a meal.

Bran, of course, should be used only by those in normal health—meaning those who are free of digestive disorders. While sufferers from diverticulosis and other digestive diseases sometimes profit by this source of bulk, they should use it only under medical supervision.

The requisite amount of bran is up to the individual. Begin with a teaspoonful once a day, after a meal; gradually increase this amount by a teaspoonful after a second meal, and so on, until you establish elimination without straining. At this point, the satiety effect should be demonstrated, too.

Multiple vitamins and minerals should accompany the low-carbohydrate diet, too, particularly if you're using bran, for this may increase your mineral requirements.

The Low-Carbohydrate Reducing Diet

In the menus for a low-carbohydrate reducing diet, there are no absolutes in choice of foods. The only rule you need to remember is that you must exchange like for like—carbohydrate for carbohydrate, protein for protein, unsaturated fat for unsaturated fat, saturated fat for saturated fat. This means you may interchange eggs for meat, meat for fish, fowl for cheese, etc.; you may choose brown-rice crackers for the whole-wheat bread, or whole-rye bread for whole-corn bread. But *don't* take more bread in exchange for less meat, *don't* substitute butter or lard for vegetable oil, and *don't* skimp on fish to "make room" for a forbidden dessert. If you do, you'll defeat your diet and stop your weight loss.

In exchanging one food for another of the same type, there *is* one thing you should be careful of. If you don't like or don't tolerate milk, yogurt, or cheese, and choose to substitute other proteins—meat, fish, or fowl—for these, you will create a deficit in calcium, which is provided by the dairy foods but is poorly supplied by other proteins. If you choose not to use dairy products, a calcium supplement—bone meal, dolomite, or calcium orotate (the most effective)—is a wise protection.

The use of salad oil in the low-carbohydrate menus is *not* optional. You may consider it strange that you are required to use about five teaspoons of such high-calorie fats daily, but unsaturated fat is needed to make the diet effective. It helps not only with weight loss but also with the loss of the bulges that ordinarily evade the effect of weight loss.

By vegetable fats I *don't* mean hydrogenated fats, even if they are of vegetable origin. I mean mayonnaise and salad oil—preferably uncooked. Wheat-germ oil is fine if you prefer it. Any other vegetable oil (*except olive oil*) is approved so long as it doesn't contain BHA or BHT.

On the low-carbohydrate diet you must avoid all forms of sugar—soft drinks, sugar-sweetened juices, sugar-packed or syrup-packed canned and frozen foods. Also avoid honey, molasses, and other foods rich in carbohydrates, such as cookies, pretzels, crackers, potato chips, cakes, and popcorn. Use salt substitutes if if you wish or if your physician instructs you to. Use sugar substitutes within reason. You may have unsweetened whole gelatin, incorporating permitted fruits in permitted amounts, as a dessert. Vinegar, spices, herbs, and lemon juice are allowed, and all make good seasonings.

If you're a compulsive late-night refrigerator raider,

drink a small glass of a dry wine an hour before dinner and an hour before bedtime. But don't drink it if you don't really need it.

Always be careful to stay within the limits of carbohydrate allowed. Interchange leafy vegetables as you choose, but don't substitute potatoes—high in starch—for spinach, which is low in starch. Fruits are relatively rich in sugar, and portions of these *must* be held to the limits set in the menus. But generally fruits are interchangeable, too, as long as they're listed as permissible.

If you don't want to add bran to your foods, you might consider taking bran tablets. Again, begin with a teaspoonful of bran a day and work your way up. A half-gram bran tablet is equal to half a teaspoonful of bran.

Typical Low-Carbohydrate Meals and Snacks

Breakfast

grapefruit half

poached egg with two pork or beef sausages (no BHA or BHT)

half a slice of whole-wheat, whole-rye, or whole-corn bread with one level teaspoonful of highly unsaturated margarine

beverage of choice—coffee or decaffeinated coffee, herb or regular tea; use cream and artificial sweetener, if desired

Morning Booster

skim milk (one cup)

creamed cottage cheese (¼ cup) with added bran, well stirred

Lunch

clear soup (optional)

chicken salad (with approximately four
ounces of chicken and one or two teaspoons mayonnaise, on lettuce, chicory, or
escarole—unlimited amounts—plus
chopped celery and sliced tomatoes)

green or wax beans or other vegetable from
approved list

brown-rice crackers (five) with ½ teaspoon
margarine, *or* brown-rice cake (obtainable
in health-food stores)

beverage of choice

Afternoon Snack

yogurt (½ cup) with added bran, well stirred

your favorite cheese (one ounce)—*not*
"cheese food"—with one small whole-
wheat cracker

Dinner

clear soup (optional)

tomato juice (four ounces)

steak (¼ pound)

cauliflower with one teaspoon margarine

tossed salad, vinegar-and-oil dressing (no
limit on salad portions)

strawberries and half-and-half (small amount)
with optional artificial sweetener

beverage of choice

Evening Snack

skim milk or yogurt (½ cup) with added bran
leftover chicken, cheese, meat, or fish (one
ounce) *or* a small portion of peanut or
other nut butter on two brown-rice crackers, one brown-rice cake, or one whole-
grain cracker

Approved Vegetables

Your vegetables will be selected from the following
list. Eat a daily minimum of two cups, total, up to a
maximum of four cups.

Vegetables marked with a dot are good sources of
Vitamin C, often rich in other nutritional values, and
should be emphasized if they please your palate. Of
course, the vitamins in your multiple-vitamin supplement will protect you even if you're determined not to
eat anything that's good for you.

asparagus	•turnip greens
avocado	lettuce
•broccoli	mushrooms
brussels sprouts	radishes
cabbage	sauerkraut
celery	string beans
chicory	•beet greens
cucumbers	•chard
escarole	•collards
eggplant	•dandelion
green pepper	endive
kohlrabi	green or wax beans
leeks	tomatoes
•kale	tomato juice
•mustard	summer squash
•spinach	watercress

Approved Fruits

Take two servings of fruit daily in amounts listed. Those marked with a dot are good sources of Vitamin C. Fresh, canned, cooked, or frozen fruits may be used, if they're free of added sugar—artificially sweetened fruit is okay, though.

All fruits and vegetables, whether served uncooked or cooked, peeled or unpeeled, should be thoroughly washed before consumption. Pesticide residues help no one, and can be reduced significantly by washing.

Fruit	*Serving*
apple	one small
applesauce	½ cup
apricots, fresh	two medium
apricots, dried	four halves
banana	one half small
blackberries	one cup
blueberries	⅔ cup
•cantaloupe	one fourth of six-inch melon
cherries	ten large
cranberries	one cup
dates	two
figs, fresh	two large
figs, dried	one small
•grapefruit	one half small
•grapefruit juice	½ cup
grapes	twelve large
grape juice	¼ cup
honeydew melon	one eighth medium
mango	one small
nectarine	one medium

Fruit	*Serving*
•orange	one small
•orange juice	½ cup
papaya	one third medium
peach	one medium
pear	one small
persimmon	one half small
pineapple	½ cup
pineapple juice	⅓ cup
plums	two medium
prunes	two medium
raspberries	one cup
rhubarb	one cup
•strawberries	one cup
tangerine	one cup
watermelon	one cup

Successful Management of the Low-Carbohydrate Diet

Take your vegetable oil on salads; don't use it for frying. There is nothing wrong with properly fried foods, but high temperatures may change the characteristics of the polyunsaturated fats—and those characteristics are important to full success with a low-carbohydrate diet.

At the beginning of the diet your objective is to keep your carbohydrate intake at about sixty grams daily. This is merely a starting point—some people lose successfully on more than sixty grams of carbohydrates; some do better if they eat even less than that. When you've gotten some experience with this diet, you can raise or lower your carbohydrate intake if you wish.

With that sixty-gram ceiling on carbohydrates, you must be careful in exchanging foods. Remember that you can't substitute an extra slice of bread or a few crackers for a few ounces of meat: like must be substituted for like. All animal proteins are alike, though the quantities needed for a given amount of protein intake may differ. A quarter of a cup of creamed or uncreamed cottage cheese, farmer cheese, or pot cheese may be substituted for an ounce of meat. About two ounces of meat, raw weight, may be replaced with an egg. An ounce of cheddar or other American-type cheese can replace about two ounces of meat, raw weight. Though peanut butter is high in protein it doesn't fit well into protein exchanges, because it's also very high in carbohydrates.

Your weight loss on the low-carbohydrate diet may be—and often is—dramatic in the first two weeks. It often slows up after that, but if the diet has been properly managed, the trend in pounds and ounces will be continuously downward. The satiety value of a high-protein, high-fat diet like this is considerable; if you also use bran, you should have no trouble in mastering your appetite.

It is very important that you check the carbohydrate values of foods in this book until you reach the stage where correct selection and correct rejection come by reflex, without much conscious thought. And keep on reading labels whether you're on the conventional low-calorie or the low-carbohydrate diet, for manufacturers frequently change their recipes, and the changes aren't always in your favor.

Where percentages or actual calorie or carbohydrate values aren't specified on a label the sequence in which the ingredients are listed will give you a clue, for they are usually in the order of percentage. If you're watching calories, the listing of "fat" as the first ingredient in a product tells you that the food contains more fat than it does anything else. The listing of "sugar" as the first ingredient is a clear warning, both for calorie counters and carbohydrate watchers.

A physician once told me that he had specialized in nutrition after he'd noticed that his pregnant patients —the only ones whose diets he then supervised—seem to benefit by his medical care than any other group. Certainly this is also true of the pregnant women for whom I have supplied diets for more than three decades but the most *immediate* dividends seem to come not to pregnant women but to people who have reduced to—and then stayed at—normal weight.

Even a few extra pounds tilt the scales away from well-being and toward a long list of common disorders. If you have the know-how to get rid of those extra pounds and then keep them off, you can do a lot for your health as well as your figure. That know-how begins with informing yourself about the calorie and carbohydrate values of everyday foods. With this book you can take an important step toward the best protection for health and well-being the average person can achieve: an understanding of a basic, important aspect of nutrition.

Notes on Calories, Carbohydrates, and the Metric System

Calories

A calorie is a unit of measurement that tells you how much energy you get from food. Your body needs energy for activity; it also needs energy even when you're at rest. Eating foods day after day that have *fewer* total calories than you use up will help you lose weight. If you eat foods that have *more* total calories than you need, the extra energy will be stored as fat—you will gain weight. *All foods provide calories,* although some provide very few.

Carbohydrates

Foods contain three types of carbohydrate starch, sugar, and cellulose. Starch and sugar give energy. You get starch from grain products (cereal, flour, bread, pasta), potatoes, and dry beans and peas. Sugar comes from sources such as cane and beet sugar, jellies, candy, honey, molasses, and syrup. Cellulose, important for bulk (roughage) in the diet, is found in fruits, vegetables, and whole-grain cereals.

Activity and Calories

The number of calories you spend each day (in addition to those spent just to keep your body functioning) depends on the kind of work you do and the kind of leisure-time activities you engage in.

Both the degree of physical exertion required by each task or activity *and* the length of time you spend on it determine the amount of energy you use.

The following chart will give you some idea of how many calories you use up during your various daily activities.

Sedentary activities

Calories per hour
80 to 100

reading, writing, eating, watching television or movies, listening to the radio, sewing, playing cards, typing normally or doing other office work, and performing other activities while sitting that require little or no arm movement

Light activities

Calories per hour
110 to 160

preparing and cooking food, doing dishes, dusting, hand washing small articles of clothing, ironing, walking slowly, typing rapidly and doing relatively strenuous office work, and performing other activities while standing that require some arm movement

Moderate activities

Calories per hour
170 to 240

making beds, mopping and scrubbing, sweeping, doing light polishing and waxing, laundering by machine, doing light gardening and carpentry work, walking moderately fast, performing other activities while standing that require moderate arm movement, and performing activities while sitting that require more vigorous arm movement

	Calories per hour
Vigorous activities	
doing heavy scrubbing and waxing, hand washing large articles of clothing, hanging out clothes, stripping beds, walking fast, bowling, golfing, gardening	250 to 350

	Calories per hour
Strenuous activities	
swimming, playing tennis, running, bicycling, dancing, skiing, playing football	350 or more

Age, Sex, Height, Weight—and Calorie Needs

Calorie needs differ depending upon the sex, age, and normal level of activity of the person in question. The chart that follows lists the amount of food energy—in calories—that men, women, and children of various ages require.

	Age in years	Food energy in calories
Children	1–3	1,300
	4–6	1,800
	7–10	2,400

	Age in years	Food energy in calories
Men	11–14	2,800
	15–18	3,000
	19–22	3,000
	23–50	2,700
	51 plus	2,400
Women	11–14	2,400
	15–18	2,100
	19–22	2,100
	23–50	2,000
	51 plus	1,800
pregnant		+300
nursing		+500

Are you overweight (or underweight)? Consult one of the following charts to find out.

Height without shoes	Weight in pounds without clothing		
Men	low	average	high
5 feet 3 inches	118	129	141
5 feet 4 inches	122	133	145
5 feet 5 inches	126	137	149
5 feet 6 inches	130	142	155
5 feet 7 inches	134	147	161
5 feet 8 inches	139	151	166
5 feet 9 inches	143	155	170
5 feet 10 inches	147	159	174
5 feet 11 inches	150	163	178
6 feet	154	167	183
6 feet 1 inch	158	171	188
6 feet 2 inches	162	175	192
6 feet 3 inches	165	178	195

Height without shoes	Weight in pounds without clothing		
Women	low	average	high
5 feet	100	109	118
5 feet 1 inch	104	112	121
5 feet 2 inches	107	115	125
5 feet 3 inches	110	118	128
5 feet 4 inches	113	122	132
5 feet 5 inches	116	125	135
5 feet 6 inches	120	129	139
5 feet 7 inches	123	132	142
5 feet 8 inches	126	136	146
5 feet 9 inches	130	140	151
5 feet 10 inches	133	144	156
5 feet 11 inches	137	148	161
6 feet	141	152	166

Height without shoes	Weight in kilograms without clothing		
Men	low	average	high
1.60 meters	53.52	58.51	63.96
1.63 meters	55.34	60.33	65.77
1.65 meters	57.15	62.14	67.59
1.68 meters	58.97	64.41	70.31
1.70 meters	60.78	66.68	73.03
1.73 meters	63.05	68.49	75.30
1.75 meters	64.86	70.31	77.11
1.78 meters	66.68	72.12	78.93
1.80 meters	68.04	73.94	80.74
1.83 meters	69.85	75.75	83.01
1.85 meters	71.67	77.57	85.28
1.88 meters	73.48	79.38	87.09
1.91 meters	74.84	80.74	88.45

Height without shoes	Weight in kilograms without clothing		
Women	*low*	*average*	*high*
1.52 meters	45.36	49.44	53.52
1.55 meters	47.18	50.80	54.89
1.58 meters	48.54	52.16	56.70
1.60 meters	49.90	53.52	58.06
1.63 meters	51.26	55.34	59.88
1.65 meters	52.62	56.70	61.24
1.68 meters	54.43	58.51	63.05
1.70 meters	55.79	59.88	64.41
1.73 meters	57.15	61.69	66.23
1.75 meters	58.97	63.50	68.49
1.78 meters	60.33	65.32	70.76
1.80 meters	62.14	67.13	73.03
1.83 meters	63.96	68.98	75.30

Metric Equivalents

English system		Metric system
teaspoon	equals	.0049 liters, or about 5 milliliters (volume)
tablespoon	equals	.0148 liters, or about 15 milliliters (volume)
cup	equals	.2368 liters, or about 237 milliliters (volume)
pint	equals	.4736 liters, or about 474 milliliters (volume)
ounce	equals	28.349 grams (weight)
pound	equals	453.592 grams (weight); 1 kilogram equals 2.2 pounds
inch	equals	2.54 centimeters (linear measure)
foot	equals	30.48 centimeters (linear measure)

Calories

Milk and Milk Products

	Measure	Calories
Milk		
whole	1 cup	160
skim	1 cup	90
partly skimmed (2 percent), nonfat milk solids added	1 cup	145
buttermilk	1 cup	90
evaporated milk, undiluted	½ cup	175
condensed milk, sweetened, undiluted	½ cup	490
Cream		
half-and-half (milk and cream)	1 tablespoon	20
light, coffee or table	1 tablespoon	30
sour cream	1 tablespoon	25
whipped topping (pressurized)	1 tablespoon	10
whipping cream, unwhipped (volume about double when whipped), light	1 tablespoon	45
whipping cream, unwhipped, heavy	1 tablespoon	55

Milk, continued	**Measure**	**Calories**
Imitation cream products (made with vegetable fat)		
creamer, powdered	1 teaspoon	10
creamer liquid (frozen)	1 tablespoon	20
sour dressing (imitation sour cream) made with nonfat dry milk	1 tablespoon	20
whipped topping; pressurized	1 tablespoon	10
whipped topping, frozen	1 tablespoon	10
whipped topping, powdered, made with whole milk	1 tablespoon	10
Cheese		
natural cheeses		
blue or Roquefort type	1 ounce	105
	1-inch cube	65
Camembert, packed in four-ounce package, three wedges per package	1 wedge	115
cheddar	1 ounce	115
	1-inch cube	70
	½ cup grated (about 2 ounces)	225
Parmesan, grated	1 tablespoon	25
	1 ounce	130
Swiss	1 ounce	105
	1-inch cube	55
pasteurized processed cheeses		
American	1 ounce	105
	1-inch cube	65

Milk, continued	Measure	Calories
Swiss	1 ounce	100
	1-inch cube	65

Milk products, continued

Cheese

American cheese food	1 tablespoon	45
	1-inch cube	55
American cheese spread	1 tablespoon	40
	1 ounce	80
cottage cheese, large or small curd	1 cup, curd packed	260
creamed	2 tablespoons (1 ounce)	30
uncreamed	1 cup, curd packed	170
	2 tablespoons (1 ounce)	20
cream cheese	1 ounce	105
	1-inch cube	60

Yogurt

made from partially skimmed milk	1 cup	125
made from whole milk	1 cup	150

Meat

Beef

pot roast, braised or simmered, lean and fat	3 ounces (1 thick or 2 thin slices about 4 x 2⅛ inches)	245
pot roast, braised or simmered, lean only	3 ounces (1 thick or 2 thin slices about 4 x 2⅛ inches)	165
oven roast cut relatively fat, such as rib; lean and fat	3 ounces (1 thick or 2 thin slices about 4 x 2¼ inches)	375

Meat, continued	Measure	Calories
oven roast cut relatively fat; lean only	3 ounces (1 thick or 2 thin slices about 4 x 2¼ inches)	205
oven roast cut relatively lean, such as round; lean and fat	3 ounces (1 thick or 2 thin slices about 4 x 2¼ inches)	220
oven roast cut relatively lean; lean only	3 ounces (1 thick or 2 thin slices about 4 x 2¼ inches)	160
steak, broiled, cut relatively fat, such as sirloin; lean and fat	3 ounces (1 piece about 3½ x 2 x ¾ inches)	330
steak, broiled, cut relatively fat, lean only	3 ounces (1 piece about 3½ x 2 x ¾ inches)	175
steak, broiled, cut relatively lean, such as round; lean and fat	3 ounces (1 piece about 4 x 2 x ½ inches)	220
steak, broiled, cut relatively lean, lean only	3 ounces (1 piece about 4 x 2 x ½ inches)	160
hamburger patty, broiled, panbroiled, or sautéed	3-ounce patty (about 2⅝ inches in diameter, ¾ inch thick)	245
lean ground beef	3-ounce patty (about 2⅝ inches in diameter, ¾ inch thick)	185
corned beef, canned	3 ounces (1 piece about 4 x 2½ x ½ inches)	185
corned beef hash, canned	3 ounces	155

Meat, continued

	Measure	Calories
dried beef, chipped	2 ounces (about ⅓ cup)	115
dried beef, creamed	½ cup	190
beef and vegetable stew, canned	1 cup	195
beef and vegetable stew, homemade, with lean beef	1 cup	220
beef pot pie, homemade	one fourth of 9-inch pie	385
chili con carne, canned, without beans	1 cup	480
chili con carne, canned, with beans	1 cup	340

Veal

	Measure	Calories
cutlet, broiled, trimmed, meat only	3 ounces (1 piece about 3¾ x 2½ x ⅜ inches)	185
roast, cooked, without bone	3 ounces (1 thick or 2 thin slices about 4 x 2¼ inches)	230

Lamb

	Measure	Calories
loin chop (about three chops to a pound, as purchased), lean and fat	3½ ounces	355
loin chop, lean only	2⅓ ounces	120
loin chop, broiled, without bone, lean and fat	3 ounces	305
loin chop, broiled, without bone; lean only	3 ounces	160
leg of lamb, roasted, lean and fat	3 ounces (1 thick or 2 thin slices about 4 x 2¼ inches)	235

Meat, continued	Measure	Calories
leg of lamb, lean only	3 ounces (1 thick or 2 thin slices about 4 x 2¼ inches)	175

Pork, fresh

chop (about three chops to a pound, as purchased), lean and fat	2⅔ ounces	305
chop, lean only	2 ounces	150
roast, loin, lean and fat	3 ounces (1 thick or 2 thin slices about 3½ x 2½ inches)	310
roast, loin, lean only	3 ounces (1 thick or 2 thin slices about 3½ x 2½ inches)	215

Pork, cured

ham, cooked, lean and fat	3 ounces (1 thick or 2 thin slices about 3½ x 2½ inches)	245
ham, cooked, lean only	3 ounces (1 thick or 2 thin slices about 3½ x 2½ inches)	160
bacon, broiled or fried crisp	2 thin slices (28 slices per pound)	60
	2 medium slices (20 slices per pound)	85
bacon, Canadian, cooked	1 slices about 3⅜ inches in diameter, ¼ inch thick	60

Sausage and variety and luncheon meats

bologna	2 ounces (2 very thin slices about 4½ inches in diameter)	170
braunschweiger	2 ounces (2 slices	

Meat, continued	Measure	Calories
	about 3⅛ inches in diameter)	180
Vienna sausage, canned	2 ounces	135
pork sausage, link	4 links 4 inches long (4 ounces, uncooked)	250
pork sausage, bulk	2 patties about 3⅞ inches in diameter, ¼ inch thick (4 ounces, uncooked)	260
beef liver, fried (including fat for frying)	3 ounces (1 piece about 6½ x 2⅜ x ⅜ inches)	195
beef heart, braised, trimmed of fat	3 ounces (1 thick piece about 4 x 2½ inches)	160
salami	2 ounces (2 slices about 4½ inches in diameter)	175
beef tongue, braised	3 ounces (1 slice about 3 x 2 x ⅜ inches)	210
frankfurter	2-ounce frankfurter	170
boiled ham (luncheon meat)	2 ounces (2 very thin slices about 6¼ x 4 inches)	135
spiced ham, canned	2 ounces (2 thin slices about 3 x 2 inches)	165

Poultry

Chicken

broiled (no skin)	3 ounces (about one fourth of a broiler)	115

Poultry, continued	Measure	Calories
fried	one half breast, 2¾ ounces, meat only	120
	1 drumstick, 1⅓ ounces, meat only	90
canned, meat only	3½ ounces (½ cup)	200
Poultry pie, homemade, one fourth of	one fourth of 9-inch pie	410

Turkey

roasted, light meat (no skin)	3 ounces (1 thick or 2 thin slices about 4¼ x 2 inches)	150
roasted, dark meat (no skin)	3 ounces (1 thick or 2 thin slices about 4¼ x 2 inches)	175

Fish and Shellfish

Blue fish, baked with fat	3 ounces (1 piece about 3½ x 2 x ½ inches)	135
Clams, shelled, raw, meat only	3 ounces (about 4 medium clams)	65
Clams, canned, clams and juice	3 ounces (1 scant ½ cup—3 medium clams and juice)	45
Crabmeat, canned or cooked	3 ounces (½ cup)	80
Fish sticks (frozen), breaded, cooked (including breading and fat for frying)	3 ounces (3 fish sticks 4 x 1 x ½ inches)	150
Haddock, breaded, fried (including fat for frying)	3 ounces (1 fillet about 4 x 2½ x ½ inches)	140

Fish, continued	Measure	Calories
Mackerel broiled with fat	3 ounces (1 piece about 4 x 3 x ½ inches)	200
Mackerel, canned	3 ounces, solids and liquids	155
Ocean perch, breaded, fried (including fat for frying)	3 ounces (1 piece about 4 x 2½ x ½ inches)	195
Oysters, raw, meat only	½ cup (6 to 10 medium-sized)	80
Salmon, broiled or baked	3 ounces	155
	4 ounces (1 steak about 4½ x 2½ x ½ inches)	205
Salmon, canned (pink)	3 ounces, solids and liquids	120
Sardines, canned in oil	3 ounces, drained solids (7 medium sardines)	170
Shrimp, canned, meat only	3 ounces (27 medium shrimp)	100
Tunafish, canned in oil	3 ounces, drained solids (¼ cup)	170

Eggs

Fried (including fat for frying)	1 large egg	100
Hard- or soft-boiled	1 large egg	80
Scrambled or omelet (including milk and fat for cooking)	1 large egg	110
Poached	1 large egg	80

Dry Beans and Peas

	Measure	Calories
Red kidney beans, canned or cooked	½ cup, solids and liquid	110
Lima beans, cooked	½ cup	130
Baked beans, canned, with pork and tomato sauce	½ cup	155
Baked beans, canned, with pork and sweet sauce	½ cup	190

Nuts

Almonds	2 tablespoons (15 almonds)	105
Brazil nuts	2 tablespoons (4 to 5 large kernels)	115
Cashew nuts, roasted	2 tablespoons (11 to 12 medium nuts)	100
Coconut, fresh, shredded meat	4 tablespoons	110
Peanuts, roasted	4 tablespoons	210
Peanut butter	1 tablespoon	95
Pecan halves	2 tablespoons (10 jumbo or 15 large)	95

Walnuts

black or native, chopped	4 tablespoons	200
English or Persian, halves	2 tablespoons (6 to 7 halves)	80

Vegetables

Asparagus, cooked or canned	6 medium spears or ½ cup cut spears	20

Vegetables, continued	Measure	Calories
Beans		
lima, cooked or canned	½ cup	90
snap—green, wax, or yellow—cooked or canned	½ cup	15
Beets, cooked or canned	½ cup diced, sliced, or small whole	30
Beet greens, cooked	½ cup	15
Broccoli, cooked	½ cup chopped, or 3 stalks 4½ to 5 inches long	25
Brussels sprouts, cooked	½ cup (4 sprouts 1¼ to 1½ inches in diameter)	25
Cabbage		
raw	½ cup shredded, chopped, or sliced	10
coleslaw with mayonnaise	½ cup	85
coleslaw with mayonnaise-type salad dressing	½ cup	60
cooked	½ cup	15
Carrots		
raw	1, about 7½ inches long, 1⅛ inches in diameter	30
	½ cup grated	25
cooked or canned	½ cup	25
Cauliflower, cooked	1 cup	30
Celery		
raw	3 inner stalks about 5 inches long	10
cooked	½ cup diced	10

Vegetables, continued	Measure	Calories
Chard, cooked	½ cup	15
Chicory, raw	½ cup	5
Chives, raw	1 tablespoon	trace
Collards, cooked	½ cup	25

Corn

on the cob, cooked	1 ear about 5 inches long, 1¾ inches in diameter	70
kernels, cooked or canned	½ cup	70
cream-style	½ cup	105
Cress, garden, cooked	½ cup	15
Cucumbers, raw, pared	6 center slices ⅛ inch thick	5
Dandelion greens, cooked	½ cup	15
Eggplant, cooked	½ cup	20
Endive, raw	½ cup	5
Kale, cooked	½ cup	20
Kohlrabi, cooked	½ cup	20
Lettuce, raw	2 large leaves	5
	½ cup shredded or chopped	5
	1 wedge—one sixth head	10
Mushrooms, canned	½ cup	20
Mustard greens, cooked	½ cup	15
Okra, cooked	½ cup cuts and pods	35
	½ cup sliced	25

Onions

young, green, raw	2 medium or 6 small, without tops	15
	1 tablespoon chopped	5
mature, raw	1 tablespoon chopped	5
mature, cooked	½ cup	30

Vegetables, continued	Measure	Calories
Parsley, raw	1 tablespoon chopped	trace
Parsnips, cooked	½ cup diced	50
	½ cup mashed	70
Peas, green, cooked or canned	½ cup	65
Peppers, green		
raw	1 ring ¼ inch thick	trace
	1 tablespoon chopped	trace
cooked	1 medium, about 2¾ inches long, 2½ inches in diameter	15
Potatoes		
baked	1, about 4¾ inches long, 2⅓ inches in diameter	145
boiled	1, about 2½ inches in diameter	90
chips	10, about 1¾ x 2½ inches	115
French-fried, fresh, cooked in deep fat	10, 3½ to 4 inches long	215
French-fried, frozen, heated, ready-to-serve	10, 3½ to 4 inches long	170
pan fried from raw	½ cup	230
hash browned	½ cup	175
mashed, milk added	½ cup	70
mashed, milk and fat added	½ cup	100

Vegetables, continued	Measure	Calories
mashed, made from granules, with milk and fat added	½ cup	100
au gratin	½ cup	180
scalloped, without cheese	½ cup	125
salad, made with cooked salad dressing	½ cup	125
salad, made with mayonnaise or French dressing and eggs	½ cup	180
sticks	½ cup	95
Pumpkin, canned	½ cup	40
Radishes, raw	4 medium	4
Rutabagas, cooked	½ cup diced or sliced	30
Sauerkraut, canned	½ cup	20
Spinach, cooked or canned	½ cup	25

Squash

summer, cooked	½ cup	15
winter, baked	½ cup mashed	65
winter, boiled	½ cup mashed	45

Sweet potatoes

baked in skin	1, about 5 inches long, 2 inches in diameter	160
candied	one half, about 2½ inches long	160
canned	½ cup mashed	140

Tomatoes

raw	1, about 2½ inches in diameter	20
cooked or canned	½ cup	30

Vegetables, continued	Measure	Calories
Tomato juice, canned	½ cup	25
Tomato juice cocktail, canned	½ cup	25
Turnips		
raw	½ cup cubed or sliced	20
cooked	½ cup diced	20
Turnip greens, cooked	½ cup	15
Vegetable juice cocktail	½ cup	20
Watercress, raw	10 sprigs	5

Fruits

Apples, raw	1 medium (about 2¾ inches in diameter)	80
Apple juice, canned	½ cup	60
Applesauce		
sweetened	½ cup	115
unsweetened	½ cup	50
Apricots		
raw	3 (about 12 per pound as purchased)	55
canned, water pack	½ cup halves and liquid	45
canned, heavy syrup pack	½ cup halves and syrup	110
dried, cooked, unsweetened	½ cup fruit and juice	105

Fruits, continued	Measure	Calories
Avocados		
California varieties	one half of 10-ounce avocado (about 3⅛ inches in diameter)	190
Florida varieties	one half of 16-ounce avocado (about 3⅝ inches in diameter)	205
Bananas, raw	1 banana 6 to 7 inches long	85
	1 banana 8 to 9 inches long	100
Blackberries, raw	½ cup	40
Blueberries		
fresh, raw	½ cup	45
frozen, sweetened	½ cup	120
frozen, unsweetened	½ cup	45
Raspberries		
fresh, red, raw	½ cup	35
frozen, red, sweetened	½ cup	120
fresh, black, raw	½ cup	50
Strawberries		
fresh, raw	½ cup	30
frozen, sweetened	½ cup sliced	140
Cantaloupe, raw	one half of melon about 5 inches in diameter	80
Cherries		
sour, raw, with pits	½ cup	30
sour, canned (water pack), pitted	½ cup	50
sweet, raw, with pits	½ cup	40

Fruits, continued	Measure	Calories
sweet, canned (water pack), with pits	½ cup	65
sweet, canned (syrup pack), with pits	½ cup	105
Cranberry sauce, sweetened, canned	2 tablespoons	50
Dates, fresh, dried, pitted, cut	½ cup	245

Figs

raw	3 small about 1½ inches in diameter (about ¼ pound)	95
canned, heavy syrup	½ cup	110
dried	1 large, about 2 x 1 inches	60
Fruit cocktail, canned in heavy syrup	½ cup	95

Grapefruit

raw, white	one half medium (about 3¾ inches in diameter)	45
raw, pink or red	one half medium (about 3¾ inches in diameter)	50
canned, water pack	½ cup	35
canned, syrup pack	½ cup	90

Grapefruit juice

fresh	½ cup	50
canned, unsweetened	½ cup	50
canned, sweetened	½ cup	65
frozen concentrate, diluted, ready-to-serve, unsweetened	½ cup	50

Fruits, continued	**Measure**	**Calories**
frozen concentrate, diluted, ready-to-serve, sweetened	½ cup	60

Grapes

American type (Concord, Delaware, Niagara, Scuppernong), slip skin	1 bunch about 3½ x 3 inches (about 3½ ounces) ½ cup	45 35
European type (Malaga, Muscat, Thompson seedless, Flame Tokay), adherent skin	½ cup	55

Grape juice

bottled	½ cup	85
frozen concentrate, diluted, ready-to-serve	½ cup	65
Honeydew melon, raw	1 wedge about 2 x 7 inches	50
Lemon juice, fresh or canned	½ cup 1 tablespoon	30 5
Lemonade, frozen concentrate, diluted, ready-to-serve	½ cup	55
Oranges, raw	1, about 2⅝ inches in diameter	65

Orange juice

fresh	½ cup	55
canned, unsweetened	½ cup	60
frozen concentrate, diluted, ready-to-serve	½ cup	55

Fruits, continued	Measure	Calories
Peaches		
raw	1 medium (about 2½ inches in diameter)	40
	½ cup sliced	30
canned, water pack	½ cup	40
canned, syrup pack	½ cup	100
dried, cooked, unsweetened	½ cup (5 to 6 halves and liquid)	100
frozen, sweetened	½ cup	110
Pears		
raw	1, about 3½ inches long, 2½ inches in diameter	100
canned, water pack	½ cup	40
canned, syrup pack	½ cup	95
Pineapple		
raw	½ cup diced	40
canned in heavy syrup —crushed, tidbits, or chunks	½ cup	95
canned in heavy syrup —sliced	2 small slices or 1 large and 2 tablespoons juice	80
Pineapple juice, canned, unsweetened	½ cup	70
Plums		
Raw, Damson	5, about 1 inch in diameter	30
raw, Japanese	1, about 2⅛ inches in diameter	30
canned (syrup pack), with pits	½ cup	105

Fruits, continued	Measure	Calories
Prunes, cooked		
unsweetened	½ cup fruit and liquid	125
sweetened	½ cup fruit and liquid	205
Prune juice, canned	½ cup	100
Raisins	½ cup, packed	240
Rhubarb, cooked, sweetened	½ cup	190
Tangerines, raw	1 medium (about 2⅜ inches in diameter)	40
Tangerine juice		
canned, unsweetened	½ cup	55
canned, sweetened	½ cup	60
Watermelon, raw	1 wedge about 4 x 8 inches	110

Breads

Cracked wheat bread	1 slice	65
Raisin bread	1 slice	65
Rye bread	1 slice	60
White bread		
soft crumb, regular slice	1 slice	70
soft crumb, thin slice	1 slice	55
firm crumb	1 slice	65
Whole-wheat bread		
soft crumb	1 slice	65
firm crumb	1 slice	60
Biscuits		
baking powder, home recipe	1, about 2 inches in diameter	105

Breads, continued	**Measure**	**Calories**
baking powder, from a mix	1, about 2 inches in diameter	90

Crackers

butter	1, about 2 inches in diameter	15
cheese	1, about 2 inches in diameter	15
graham	4 small or 2 medium	55
saltine	4, about 1⅞ inches square	50
matzoh	1, about 6 inches in diameter	80
pilot	1	75
oyster	10	35
rye	2, about 1⅞ x 3½ inches	45
Danish pastry, plain	1, about 4½ inches in diameter	275

Doughnuts

cake-type, plain	1, about 3¼ inches in diameter	165
yeast-leavened, raised	1, about 3¾ inches in diameter	175

Muffins

plain	1, about 3 inches in diameter	120
blueberry	1, about 2⅜ inches in diameter	110
bran	1, about 2⅝ inches in diameter	105
corn	1, about 2⅜ inches in diameter	125

Breads, continued	Measure	Calories
Pancakes		
wheat (home recipe or mix)	1, about 4 inches in diameter	60
buckwheat (made with buckwheat pancake mix)	1, about 4 inches in diameter	55
Pizza (cheese)	5½-inch sector (one eighth of 14-inch pie)	155
Pretzels, Dutch, twisted	1	60
Pretzels, stick	5 regular (3⅛ inches long) or 10 small (2¼ inches long)	10
Rolls		
hamburgers or frankfurter	1 roll (16 per pound)	120
hard, round or rectangular	1 roll (9 per pound)	155
plain, pan	1 roll (16 per pound)	85
sweet, pan	1 roll (11 per pound)	135
Waffles	1, about 7 inches in diameter	210
Spoonbread	½ cup	235

Cereals and Other Grain Products

Bran flakes (40 percent bran)	1 cup	106
Bran flakes with raisins	1 cup	135
Corn, puffed, presweetened	1 cup	115
Corn, shredded	1 cup	96

Cereals, continued	Measure	Calories
Corn flakes	1 cup	96
Corn flakes, sugar-coated	⅔ cup	110
Corn grits, degermed, cooked	¾ cup	95
Farina, cooked (quick-cooking)	¾ cup	80
Macaroni, cooked	¾ cup	115
Macaroni and cheese		
homemade	½ cup	215
canned	½ cup	115
Noodles, cooked	¾ cup	150
Oats, puffed	1 cup	99
Oats, puffed, sugar-coated	1 cup	144
Oatmeal or rolled oats, cooked	¾ cup	100
Rice, "instant," ready-to-serve	¾ cup	135
Rice flakes	1 cup	110
Rice, puffed	1 cup	57
Rice, puffed, presweetened	⅔ cup	110
Rice, shredded	1 cup	104
Spaghetti, cooked	¾ cup	115
Spaghetti with meat balls		
home recipe	¾ cup	250
canned	¾ cup	195
Spaghetti in tomato sauce		
with cheese, home recipe	¾ cup	195
with cheese, canned	¾ cup	140
Wheat, puffed	1 cup	56
Wheat, puffed, presweetened	1 cup	131
Wheat, rolled, cooked	¾ cup	135

Cereals, continued	**Measure**	**Calories**
Wheat, shredded, plain (long, round, or bite-size)	1 ounce (1 large biscuit or ½ cup bite-size)	100
Wheat flakes	1 cup	100
Wheat flours		
whole wheat	1 cup stirred	400
all-purpose	1 cup sifted	420
Wheat germ, toasted	1 tablespoon	25

Desserts

Apple Betty	½ cup	160
Brownie, with nuts	1, about 1¾ inches square, ⅞ inch thick	90
Cakes		
angel food cake	2½-inch piece (one twelfth of 9¾-inch round cake)	135
butter cake, plain, without icing	1 piece about 3 x 3 x 2 inches	315
	1 cupcake about 2¾ inches in diameter	115
butter cake, plain, with chocolate icing	1¾-inch piece (one sixteenth of 9-inch round layer cake)	240
	1 cupcake about 2¾ inches in diameter	170
chocolate, with chocolate icing	1¾-inch piece (one sixteenth of 9-inch round layer cake)	235
fruitcake, dark	1 piece about 2 x 1½ x ¼ inches	55

Desserts, continued	**Measure**	**Calories**
gingerbread	1 piece about 2¾ x 2¾ x 1⅜ inches	175
pound cake, old-fashioned	1 slice about 3½ x 3½ inches	140
sponge cake	1⅞-inch piece (one sixteenth of 9¾-inch round cake)	145

Cookies

chocolate chip	1, about 2½ inches in diameter	50
figbars	1 small	50
sandwich, chocolate or vanilla	1, about 1¾ inches in diameter	50
sugar	1, about 2¼ inches in diameter	35
vanilla wafer	1, about 1¾ inches in diameter	20
Custard, baked	½ cup	150
Fruit ice	½ cup	125

Gelatin desserts
(ready-to-serve)

plain	½ cup	70
fruit added	½ cup	80

Ice cream

regular (about 10 percent fat)	½ cup	130
rich (about 16 percent fat)	½ cup	165

Ice milk

hardened	½ cup	100
soft serve	½ cup	135

Desserts, continued	Measure	Calories
Pies		
apple	one eighth of 9-inch pie	300
blueberry	one eighth of 9-inch pie	285
Boston cream pie	2⅛-inch sector of 8-inch round cake	210
cherry	one eighth of 9-inch pie	310
chocolate meringue	one eighth of 9-inch pie	285
coconut custard	one eighth of 9-inch pie	270
custard, plain	one eighth of 9-inch pie	250
lemon meringue	one eighth of 9-inch pie	270
mince	one eighth of 9-inch pie	320
peach	one eighth of 9-inch pie	300
pecan	one eighth of 9-inch pie	430
pumpkin	one eighth of 9-inch pie	240
raisin	one eighth of 9-inch pie	320
rhubarb	one eighth of 9-inch pie	300
strawberry	one eighth of 9-inch pie	185
Prune whip	½ cup	70
Puddings		
cornstarch, vanilla	½ cup	140

Desserts, continued	Measure	Calories
chocolate, from a mix	½ cup	160
bread pudding, with raisins	½ cup	250
rennet desserts, ready-to-serve	½ cup	115
tapioca cream	½ cup	110
Sherbet	½ cup	130

Fats, Oils, and Related Products

Butter or margarine	1 tablespoon	100
	1 pat 1 inch square, ¼ inch thick	35
Margarine, whipped	1 tablespoon	70
	1 pat 1¼ inches square, ¼ inch thick	25

Cooking fats
vegetable	1 tablespoon	110
lard	1 tablespoon	115
Salad or cooking oils	1 tablespoon	120

Salad dressings, regular
blue cheese	1 tablespoon	75
French	1 tablespoon	65
home-cooked, boiled	1 tablespoon	25
Italian	1 tablespoon	85
mayonnaise	1 tablespoon	100
mayonnaise-type, commercial, plain	1 tablespoon	65
Russian	1 tablespoon	75
thousand island	1 tablespoon	80

Fats, Oils, continued	Measure	Calories
Salad dressings, low-calorie		
French	1 tablespoon	15
Italian	1 tablespoon	10
thousand island	1 tablespoon	25

Soups

Bean with pork	1 cup	170
Beef noodle	1 cup	65
Bouillon, broth, and con-somme	1 cup	30
Chicken gumbo	1 cup	55
Chicken noodle	1 cup	60
Chicken with rice	1 cup	50
Clam chowder		
Manhattan	1 cup	80
New England	1 cup	135
Cream of asparagus		
with water	1 cup	65
with milk	1 cup	145
Cream of chicken		
with water	1 cup	95
with milk	1 cup	180
Cream of mushroom		
with water	1 cup	135
with milk	1 cup	215
Minestrone	1 cup	105
Oyster stew (frozen)		
with water	1 cup	120
with milk	1 cup	200
Split pea	1 cup	145

Soups, continued	Measure	Calories
Tomato		
with water	1 cup	90
with milk	1 cup	170
Vegetable with broth	1 cup	80

Sugars, Sweets, and Related Products

Caramels	1 ounce (3 medium caramels)	115
Chocolate creams	1 ounce (2 to 3 pieces—35 to a pound)	125
Milk chocolate, sweetened	1-ounce bar	145
Milk chocolate, sweetened, with almonds	1-ounce bar	150
Chocolate mints	1 ounce (1 to 2 mints—20 to a pound)	115
Candy corn	1 ounce (20 pieces)	105
Mints	1 ounce (3 mints about 1½ inches in diameter)	105
Fudge (vanilla or chocolate)		
plain	1 ounce	115
with nuts	1 ounce	120
Gumdrops	1 ounce (2 to 3 large or about 20 small)	100
Hard candy	1 ounce (3 to 4 candy balls about ¾ inch in diameter)	110
Jelly beans	1 ounce (10 beans)	105

Sweets, continued	Measure	Calories
Marshmallows	1 ounce (4 marsh-mallows—63 to a pound)	90
Peanut brittle	1 ounce (1 to 2 pieces about 2½ × 1¼ × ⅜ inches)	120

Chocolate syrup

	Measure	Calories
thin type	1 tablespoon	45
fudge type	1 tablespoon	60
Honey, strained or extracted	1 tablespoon	65
Molasses, cane, light	1 tablespoon	50
Syrup, table blends	1 tablespoon	55
Jams, preserves	1 tablespoon	55
Jellies, marmalades	1 tablespoon	50
Sugar—white, granulated, or brown, packed	1 teaspoon	15

Beverages

Alcoholic beverages

	Measure	Calories
beer, 3.6 percent alcohol by weight	8 ounces	100 / 150
gin, rum, whisky, vodka		
100-proof	1½ ounces	125
90-proof	1½ ounces	110
86-proof	1½ ounces	105
80-proof	1½ ounces	95
table wines (such as Chablis, claret, Rhine wine, sauterne)	3½ ounces	85
dessert wines (such as muscatel, port, sherry, Tokay)	3½ ounces	140

Beverages, continued	Measure	Calories
Carbonated beverages		
ginger ale	12 ounces	115
cola-type	12 ounces	145
fruit-flavored soda (10 to 13 percent sugar)	12 ounces	170
root beer	12 ounces	150

Check labels of low-calorie soft drinks for number of calories they contain.

Fruit drinks		
apricot nectar	½ cup	70
cranberry juice cocktail, canned	½ cup	80
grape drink	½ cup	70
lemonade, frozen concentrate, diluted, ready-to-serve	½ cup	55
orange-apricot juice drink	½ cup	60
peach drink	½ cup	60
pear nectar	½ cup	65
pineapple-grapefruit juice drink	½ cup	70
pineapple-orange juice drink	½ cup	70
Fruit juices		
apple juice, canned	½ cup	60
grape juice, bottled	½ cup	85
grape juice, frozen concentrate, diluted, ready-to-serve	½ cup	65
grapefruit juice fresh	½ cup	50

Beverages, continued	Measure	Calories
canned, unsweetened	½ cup	50
canned, sweetened	½ cup	65
frozen concentrate, diluted, ready-to-serve, unsweetened	½ cup	50
frozen concentrate, ready-to-serve, sweetened	½ cup	60
lemon juice, fresh or canned	1 tablespoon	5
orange juice		
fresh	½ cup	55
canned, unsweetened	½ cup	60
frozen concentrate, diluted, ready-to-serve	½ cup	55
pineapple juice, canned, unsweetened	½ cup	70
prune juice, canned	½ cup	100
tangerine juice, canned, unsweetened	½ cup	55
tangerine juice, canned, sweetened	½ cup	60

Milk beverages

	Measure	Calories
chocolate milk, home-made	1 cup	240
cocoa, homemade	1 cup	245
chocolate-flavored drink made with skim milk	1 cup	190
chocolate-flavored drink	1 cup	215
malted milk	1 cup	245
chocolate milkshake	12 ounces	515

Snacks and Extras

	Measure	Calories
Bouillon cube	½-inch cube	5
Olives, green	5 small, 3 large, or 2 giant	15
Olives, ripe	3 small or 2 large	15
Pickles, cucumber		
dill	1, about 4 inches long, 1¾ inches in diameter	15
sweet	1, about 2½ inches long, ¾ inch in diameter	20
Popcorn, popped (with oil and salt added)	1 cup large kernels	40
Potato chips	10, about 1¾ × 2½ inches	115
Pretzels, Dutch, twisted	1	60
Pretzels, stick	5 regular (3⅛ inches long) or 10 small (2¼ inches long)	10
Chili sauce, tomato	1 tablespoon	15
Tomato catsup	1 tablespoon	15
Gravy	2 tablespoons	35
White sauce, medium (made with 1 cup milk to 2 tablespoons fat and 2 tablespoons flour)	½ cup	200
Cheese sauce (medium white sauce, above, with 2 tablespoons grated cheese per cup of sauce)	½ cup	205
Corn chips	1 cup	230

Snacks, continued	Measure	Calories

Doughnuts

cake-type, plain	1, about 3¼ inches in diameter	165
yeast-leavened, raised	1, about 3¾ inches in diameter	175

French fries

fresh, cooked in deep fat	10, 3½ to 4 inches long	215
frozen, heated, ready-to-serve	10, 3½ to 4 inches long	170
Hamburger	2-ounce meat patty, with roll	280
Hot dog —	1 average, with roll	290

Miscellaneous

Artichokes, globe or French, boiled	1	12 to 67 (depends upon whether fresh or stored)
Bamboo shoots, raw	1 pound or approximately 3 cups of 1-inch pieces	122

Caviar, sturgeon

granular	1 tablespoon	42
pressed	1 tablespoon	54
Limburger cheese	1 ounce	98
Chestnuts	10	141
Chewing gum, candy-coated	1 piece	5
Chop suey, with meat, no noodles, made from home recipe	1 cup	300

Miscellaneous, continued	Measure	Calories
Chow mein, chicken, no noodles, made from home recipe	1 cup	255
Chow mein, canned	1 cup	95
Herring		
in tomato sauce	1 herring with 1 tablespoon sauce	97
pickled	1 herring	112
smoked, kippered, drained	1 7-inch fillet	137
Lobster Newburg	1 cup	485
Loquats, raw	10	59
Lychees, raw	10	58
Mangoes, raw	1	152
Pâté de foie gras, canned	1 tablespoon	60
Persimmons		
Japanese or kaki	1	129
native	1	31
Pigs' feet, pickled	2 ounces	113
Pine nuts		
Pignolias	1 ounce	156
piñon	1 ounce	180
Plantains (baking bananas), raw	1	313
Rabbit, domesticated, flesh only, stewed	1 cup	302
Sunflower seed kernels, dry	¼ cup	203
Welsh rarebit	1 cup	415

Carbohydrates

Milk and Milk Products

	Measure	Grams Carbohydrate
Milk		
whole	1 cup	12
skim	1 cup	12
partly skimmed (2 percent), nonfat milk solids added	1 cup	15
buttermilk	1 cup	12
Evaporated milk, undiluted	½ cup	12
Condensed milk, sweetened, undiluted	½ cup	83
nonfat dry milk, instant; low-density (1⅓ cups needed to prepare one quart)	1 cup	35
nonfat dry milk, instant; high-density (⅞ cup needed to prepare one quart)	1 cup	54
Cream		
half-and-half (milk and cream)	1 tablespoon	1

Milk, continued	Measure	Grams Carbohydrate
light, coffee or table	1 tablespoon	1
sour cream	1 tablespoon	1
whipped topping (pressurized)	1 tablespoon	trace
whipping cream, unwhipped (volume about double when whipped), light	1 tablespoon	1
whipping cream, unwhipped, heavy	1 tablespoon	1

Imitation cream products
(made with vegetable fat)

creamer, powdered	1 teaspoon	1
creamer, liquid (frozen)	1 tablespoon	2
sour dressing (imitation sour cream) made with nonfat dry milk	1 tablespoon	1
whipped topping, pressurized	1 tablespoon	trace
whipped topping, frozen	1 tablespoon	1
whipped topping, powdered, made with whole milk	1 tablespoon	1

Cheese

natural cheeses		
blue or Roquefort type	1 ounce	1
	1-inch cube	trace

Milk, continued	Measure	Grams Carbohydrate
Camembert, packed in four-ounce package, three wedges per package	1 wedge	1
cheddar	1 ounce	1
	1-inch cube	trace
	½ cup grated (about 2 ounces)	2
Parmesan, grated	1 tablespoon	trace
	1 ounce	1
Swiss	1 ounce	1
	1-inch cube	trace
pasteurized processed cheeses		
American	1 ounce	1
	1-inch cube	trace
Swiss	1 ounce	1
	1-inch cube	trace
American cheese food	1 tablespoon	1
	1-inch cube	1
American cheese spread	1 ounce	2
cottage cheese, large or small curd		
creamed	1 cup, curd packed	7
uncreamed	1 cup, curd packed	6
cream cheese	1 8-ounce package	5
	1-inch cube	trace

Yogurt

made from partially skimmed milk	1 cup	13
made from whole milk	1 cup	12

Meat

	Measure	Grams Carbohydrate
Beef		
pot roast, braised or simmered, lean and fat	3 ounces (1 thick or 2 thin slices about 4 x 2⅛ inches)	0
pot roast, braised or simmered, lean only	3 ounces (1 thick or 2 thin slices about 4 x 2⅛ inches)	0
oven roast cut relatively fat, such as rib; lean and fat	3 ounces (1 thick or 2 thin slices about 4 × 2¼ inches)	0
oven roast cut relatively fat; lean only	3 ounces (1 thick or 2 thin slices about 4 x 2¼ inches)	0
oven roast cut relatively lean, such as round; lean and fat	3 ounces (1 thick or 2 thin slices about 4 x 2¼ inches)	0
oven roast cut relatively lean, lean only	3 ounces (1 thick or 2 thin slices about 4 x 2¼ inches)	0
steak, broiled, cut relatively fat, such as sirloin; lean and fat	3 ounces (1 piece about 3½ x 2 x ¾ inches)	0
steak broiled, cut relatively fat; lean only	3 ounces (1 piece about 3½ x 2 x ¾ inches)	0
steak, broiled, cut relatively lean, such as round; lean and fat	3 ounces (1 piece about 4 x 2 x ½ inches)	0
steak, broiled, cut relatively lean; lean only	3 ounces (1 piece about 4 x 2 x ½ inches)	0
hamburger patty, broiled, panbroiled,	3-ounce patty (about 2⅝ inches in di-	

Meat, continued	Measure	Grams Carbohydrate
or sautéed	ameter, ¾ inch thick)	0
lean ground beef	3-ounce patty (about 2⅝ inches in diameter, ¾ inch thick)	0
corned beef, canned	3 ounces (1 piece about 4 x 2½ x ½ inches)	0
corned beef hash, canned	3 ounces	9
dried beef, chipped	2 ounces (about ⅓ cup)	0
beef and vegetable stew, canned	1 cup	15
beef and vegetable stew, homemade, with lean beef	1 cup	15
beef pot pie	1 (4¼ inches in diameter)	43
chili con carne, canned, without beans	1 cup	15
chili con carne, canned, with beans	1 cup	30

Veal

cutlet, broiled, trimmed, meat only	3 ounces (1 piece about 3¾ x 2½ x ⅜ inches)	0
roast, cooked, without bone	3 ounces (1 thick or 2 thin slices about 4 x 2¼ inches)	0

Meat, continued	Measure	Grams Carbohydrate
Lamb		
loin chop (about three chops to a pound, as purchased), lean and fat	3½ ounces	0
loin chop, lean only	2⅓ ounces	0
leg of lamb, roasted, lean and fat	3 ounces (1 thick or 2 thin slices about 4 x 2¼ inches)	0
leg of lamb, lean only	3 ounces (1 thick or 2 thin slices about 4 x 2¼ inches)	0
Pork, fresh		
chop (about three chops to a pound, as purchased), lean and fat	2⅔ ounces	0
chop, lean only	2 ounces	0
roast, loin, lean and fat	3 ounces (1 thick or 2 thin slices about 3½ x 2½ inches)	0
roast, loin, lean only	3 ounces (1 thick or 2 thin slices about 3½ x 2½ inches)	0
Pork, cured		
ham, cooked, lean and fat	3 ounces (1 thick or 2 thin slices about 3½ x 2½ inches)	0
ham, cooked, lean only	3 ounces (1 thick or 2 thin slices about 3½ × 2½ inches)	0
bacon, broiled or fried crisp	2 medium slices (20 slices per pound)	1

Meat, continued	Measure	Grams Carbohydrate

Sausage and variety and luncheon meats

bologna	2 ounces (2 very thin slices about 4½ inches in diameter)	trace
braunschweiger	2 ounces (2 slices about 3⅛ inches in diameter)	1
Vienna sausage, canned	2 ounces	1
pork sausage, link	4 links 4 inches long (4 ounces, uncooked)	trace
pork sausage, bulk	2 patties about 3⅞ inches in diameter, ¼ inch thick (4 ounces, uncooked)	trace
beef liver, fried (including fat for frying)	3 ounces (1 piece about 6½ x 2⅜ x ⅜ inches)	4
beef heart, braised, trimmed of fat	3 ounces (1 thick piece about 4 x 2½ inches)	1
salami	2 ounces (2 slices about 4½ inches in diameter)	trace
frankfurter	2-ounce frankfurter	0
boiled ham (luncheon meat)	2 ounces (2 very thin slices about 6¼ x 4 inches)	0
spiced ham, canned	2 ounces (2 thin slices about 3 x 2 inches)	1
deviled ham, canned	1 tablespoon	trace

Poultry

	Measure	Grams Carbohydrate
Chicken		
broiled (no skin)	3 ounces (about one fourth of a broiler)	0
fried	one half breast, 2¾ ounces, meat only	1
	1 drumstick, 1⅓ ounces, meat only	trace
canned, meat only	3½ ounces (½ cup)	0
pot pie	1 (4¼ inches in diameter)	42
Turkey		
roasted, light meat (no skin)	3 ounces (1 thick or 2 thin slices about 4¼ x 2 inches)	0
roasted, dark meat (no skin)	3 ounces (1 thick or 2 thin slices about 4½ x 2inches)	0

Fish and Shellfish

Bluefish, baked with fat	3 ounces (1 piece about 3½ × 2 × ½ inches)	2
Clams, shelled, raw, meat only	3 ounces (about 4 medium clams)	2
Clams, canned, clams and juice	3 ounces (1 scant ½ cup—3 medium clams and juice)	2
Crabmeat, canned or cooked	3 ounces (½ cup)	1

Fish, continued	Measure	Grams Carbohydrate
Fish sticks (frozen), breaded, cooked (including breading and fat for frying)	3 ounces (3 fish sticks 4 x 1 x ½ inches)	5
Haddock, breaded, fried (including fat for frying)	3 ounces (1 fillet about 4 x 2½ x ½ inches)	5
Ocean perch, breaded, fried (including fat for frying)	3 ounces (1 piece about 4 x 2½ x ½ inches	6
Oysters, raw, meat only	½ cup (6 to 10 medium-sized)	4
Salmon, canned (pink)	3 ounces, solids and liquids	0
Sardines, canned in oil	3 ounces, drained solids (7 medium sardines)	0
Shad, baked with fat and bacon	3 ounces	0
Shrimp, canned, meat only	3 ounces (27 medium shrimp)	1
Swordfish, broiled with fat	3 ounces	0
Tunafish, canned in oil	3 ounces, drained solids (¼ cup)	0

Eggs

Fried (including fat for frying)	1 large egg	1
Hard- or soft-boiled	1 large egg	trace
Egg white	1	trace
Egg yolk	1	trace

Eggs, continued	Measure	Grams Carbohydrate
Scrambled or omelet (including milk and fat for cooking)	1 large egg	1
Poached	1 large egg	trace

Dry Beans and Peas

Great Northern beans, cooked	1 cup	38
Navy (pea) beans, cooked	1 cup	40
Cowpeas or blackeye peas, cooked	1 cup	34
Split peas, cooked	1 cup	52
Red kidney beans, canned or cooked	½ cup, solids and liquid	21
Lima beans, cooked	½ cup	25
Baked beans, canned, with pork and tomato sauce	½ cup	25
Baked beans, canned, with pork and sweet sauce	½ cup	27

Nuts

Almonds	2 tablespoons (15 almonds)	4
Cashew nuts, roasted	2 tablespoons (11 to 12 medium nuts)	5
Coconut, fresh, shredded meat	4 tablespoons	12
Peanuts, roasted	4 tablespoons	7

Nuts, continued	Measure	Grams Carbohydrate
Peanut butter	1 tablespoon	3
Pecan halves	2 tablespoons (10 jumbo or 15 large)	2
Walnuts, black or native, chopped	4 tablespoons	5

Vegetables

Asparagus, cooked or canned	6 medium spears or ½ cup cut spears	3

Beans

lima, cooked or canned	½ cup	17
snap—green, wax, or yellow—cooked	1 cup	7
snap—green, wax, or yellow—canned	1 cup	10

Beets

cooked	½ cup	6
canned	½ cup	10
Beet greens, cooked	1 cup	5
Broccoli, cooked	½ cup chopped	4
	1 stalk 4½ to 5 inches long	8
Brussels sprouts, cooked	½ cup (4 sprouts 1¼ to 1½ inches in diameter)	5

Cabbage

raw	½ cup shredded, chopped, or sliced	4

Vegetables, continued	Measure	Grams Carbohydrate
cooked	½ cup	3
red cabbage, raw	1 cup coarsely shredded	5
Savoy cabbage, raw	1 cup coarsely shredded	3
Chinese cabbage, raw	1 cup of 1-inch pieces	2

Carrots

raw	1, about 7½ inches long, 1⅛ inches in diameter	6
	½ cup, grated	6
cooked	½ cup	5
Cauliflower, cooked	1 cup	5

Celery

raw	3 inner stalks about 5 inches long	4
cooked	½ cup, diced	2
Collards, cooked	1 cup	9

Corn

on the cob, cooked	1 ear about 5 inches long, 1¾ inches in diameter	16
kernels, cooked or canned	½ cup	20
Cucumbers, raw, pared	6 center slices ⅛ inch thick	2
Dandelion greens, cooked	½ cup	6
Endive, raw	½ cup	2
Kale, cooked	½ cup	2

Vegetables, continued	Measure	Grams Carbohydrate
Lettuce		
raw, iceberg	1 wedge—one sixth head	2
loose-leaf types (such as romaine)	2 large leaves	2
butter-head types (such as Boston)	1 4-inch head	6
Mushrooms, canned	½ cup	3
Mustard greens, cooked	½ cup	3
Okra, cooked	8 pods	5
Onions		
young, green, raw	2 medium or 6 small, without tops	5
mature, raw	1 about 2½ inches in diameter	10
mature, cooked	½ cup	7
Parsley, raw	1 tablespoon chopped	trace
Parsnips, cooked	1 cup	23
Peas, green		
cooked	1 cup	19
canned	1 cup	31
Peppers, green		
raw	2 rings ¼ inch thick	1
	1 tablespoon chopped	trace
cooked	1 medium, about 2¾ inches long, 2½ inches in diameter	3
Pepper, hot red, without seeds, dried (with ground chili powder and added seasonings)	1 tablespoon	8

Miscellaneous, continued	Measure	Grams Carbohydrate
Potatoes		
baked	1, about 4¾ inches long, 2⅓ inches in diameter	21
boiled, peeled after boiling	1, about 2½ inches in diameter	23
boiled, peeled before boiling	1, about 2½ inches in diameter	18
chips	10, about 1¾ x 2½ inches	10
French-fried, fresh, cooked in deep fat	10, about 2 inches long	20
French-fried, frozen, heated, ready-to-serve	10, about 2 inches long	19
mashed, milk added	1 cup	25
mashed, milk and fat added	1 cup	24
Pumpkin, canned	½ cup	9
Radishes, raw	4 medium	1
Sauerkraut, canned	1 cup	9
Spinach, cooked or canned	½ cup	3
Squash		
summer, cooked	1 cup	7
winter, baked	½ cup mashed	16
Sweet potatoes		
baked in skin	1, about 5 inches long, 2 inches in diameter	36
boiled, peeled after boiling	1, about 5 inches long, 2 inches in diameter	39

Vegetables, continued	Measure	Grams Carbohydrate
candied	one half, about 2½ inches long	30
canned	½ cup mashed	27

Tomatoes

raw	1, about 2½ inches in diameter	9
cooked or canned	½ cup	5
Tomato juice, canned	½ cup	5
Turnips, cooked	½ cup diced	4
Turnip greens, cooked	1 cup	5

Fruits

Apples, raw	1 medium (about 2¾ inches in diameter)	18
Apple juice, canned	½ cup	15

Applesauce

sweetened	½ cup	30
unsweetened	½ cup	13

Apricots

raw	3 (about 12 per pound as purchased)	14
canned, heavy syrup pack	1 cup halves and syrup	57
dried, cooked, un- sweetened	½ cup fruit and juice	31
dried, uncooked	20 halves	50

Avocados

California varieties	10-ounce avocado (about 3⅛ inches in diameter)	27

Fruits, continued	Measure	Grams Carbohydrate
Florida varieties	16-ounce avocado (about 3⅝ inches in diameter)	27
Bananas, raw	1	26
Banana flakes	1 cup	89
Blackberries, raw	1 cup	19
Blueberries, raw	1 cup	21
Raspberries		
fresh, red, raw	1 cup	17
frozen, red, sweetened	½ cup	40
Strawberries		
fresh, raw	1 cup	13
frozen, sweetened	½ cup sliced	31
Cantaloupe, raw	one half of melon about 5 inches in diameter	14
Cherries, sour, canned (water pack), pitted	½ cup	13
Cranberry sauce, sweetened, canned	¼ cup	26
Dates, fresh, dried, pitted, cut	½ cup	65
Figs, dried	1 large, about 2 x 1 inches	15
Fruit cocktail, canned in heavy syrup	½ cup	25
Grapefruit		
raw, white	one half medium (about 3¾ inches in diameter)	12
raw, pink or red	one half medium (about 3¾ inches in diameter)	13

Fruits, continued	Measure	Grams Carbohydrate
canned, syrup pack	1 cup	45
Grapefruit juice		
fresh	1 cup	23
canned, unsweetened	1 cup	24
canned, sweetened	1 cup	32
frozen concentrate, diluted, ready-to-serve, unsweetened	1 cup	24
made from dehydrated crystals and water	1 cup	24
Grapes		
American type (Concord, Delaware, Niagara, Scuppernong), slip skin	1 cup	15
European type (Malaga, Muscat, Thompson seedless, Flame Tokay), adherent skin	1 cup	25
Grape juice		
bottled	½ cup	21
frozen concentrate, diluted, ready-to-serve	1 cup	33
Grape juice drink, canned	1 cup	35
Lemons, raw	1, about 2⅛ inches in diameter	6
Lemon juice, fresh or canned	½ cup	10
Lemonade, frozen concentrate, diluted, ready-to-serve	1 cup	28

Fruits, continued	Measure	Grams Carbohydrate
Lime juice, fresh or canned	½ cup	11
Limeade, frozen concentrate, diluted, ready-to-serve	1 cup	27
Oranges, raw	1, about 2⅝ inches in diameter	16
Orange juice		
fresh	½ cup	13
canned, unsweetened	½ cup	14
frozen concentrate, diluted, ready-to-serve	1 cup	29
made from dehydrated crystals and water	1 cup	27
Papayas, raw	1 cup of ½-inch cubes	18
Peaches		
raw	1 medium (about 2½ inches in diameter)	10
	½ cup sliced	8
canned, water pack	½ cup	10
canned, syrup pack	½ cup	26
dried, cooked, unsweetened	½ cup (5 to 6 halves and liquid)	29
dried, uncooked	1 cup	109
frozen, sweetened	½ cup	26
Pears		
raw	1, about 3½ inches long, 2½ inches in diameter	25
canned, syrup pack	½ cup	25

Fruits, continued	Measure	Grams Carbohydrate
Pineapple		
raw	1 cup diced	19
canned in heavy syrup —crushed, tidbits, or chunks	½ cup	25
canned in heavy syrup —sliced	2 small slices or 1 large	24
Pineapple juice, canned	½ cup	17
Plums		
raw	1, about 2 inches in diameter	7
canned (syrup pack), with pits	1 cup	53
Prunes		
cooked, unsweetened	½ cup fruit and liquid	39
uncooked	4	18
Prune juice, canned	1 cup	49
Raisins	½ cup, packed	64
Rhubarb, cooked, sweetened	½ cup	49
Tangerines, raw	1 medium (about 2⅜ inches in diameter)	10
Tangerine juice, canned, sweetened	½ cup	15
Watermelon, raw	1 wedge about 4 x 8 inches	27

Breads

Boston brown bread	1 slice 3 x ¾ inches	22
Cracked wheat bread	1 slice	13

Breads, continued	Measure	Grams Carbohydrate
Raisin bread	1 slice	13
Rye bread	1 slice	13
Pumpernickel	1 slice	13
White bread		
soft crumb, regular slice	1 slice	13
soft crumb, thin slice	1 slice	10
firm crumb	1 slice	12
Whole-wheat bread		
soft crumb	1 slice	14
firm crumb	1 slice	12
French, Italian, or Vienna bread	1 slice	14
Biscuits		
baking powder, home recipe	1, about 2 inches in diameter	13
baking powder, from a mix	1, about 2 inches in diameter	15
Bagels		
egg bagel	1	28
water bagel	1	30
Crackers		
rye	2, about 1⅞ x 3½ inches	10
graham	4 small or 2 medium	21
saltine	4, about 1⅞ inches square	8
Danish pastry, plain (without fruit or nuts)		
packaged ring	12-ounce ring	155

Breads, continued	Measure	Grams Carbohydrate
single piece	1, about 4¼ x 1 inches	30
Doughnuts, cake-type, plain	1, about 3¼ inches in diameter	16
Muffins		
plain	1, about 3 inches in diameter	17
corn	1, about 2⅜ inches in diameter	20
Pancakes		
wheat (home recipe or mix)	1, about 4 inches in diameter	9
buckwheat (made with buckwheat pancake mix)	1, about 4 inches in diameter	6
Pizza (cheese)	5½-inch piece (one eighth of 14-inch pie)	27
Pretzels, Dutch, twisted	1	12
Pretzels, stick	5 regular (3⅛ inches long) or 10 small (2¼ inches long)	2
Rolls		
hamburger or frankfurter	1 roll (16 per pound)	21
hard, round or rectangular	1 roll (9 per pound)	30
plain, pan—home recipe	1 roll	20
plain, pan—commercial	1 roll	15
Waffles	1, about 7 inches in diameter	28
Bread crumbs, dry	1 cup	73

Cereals and Other Grain Products

	Measure	Grams Carbohydrate
Bran flakes (40 percent bran)	1 cup	28
Bran flakes with raisins	1 cup	40
Corn, puffed, presweetened	1 cup	27
Corn, shredded	1 cup	25
Corn flakes	1 cup	21
Corn flakes, sugar-coated	⅔ cup	24
Corn grits, degermed, cooked	1 cup	27
Cornmeal, dry	1 cup	91
Farina, cooked (quick-cooking)	1 cup	22
Macaroni, cooked	¾ cup	24
Macaroni and cheese		
homemade	½ cup	20
canned	½ cup	13
Noodles, cooked	1 cup	37
Oats, puffed	1 cup	19
Oatmeal or rolled oats, cooked	1 cup	23
Rice		
regular enriched or unenriched, cooked	1 cup	50
"instant," ready-to-serve	1 cup	40
Rice, puffed	1 cup	13
Spaghetti, cooked	¾ cup	24
Spaghetti with meat balls		
home recipe	1 cup	39
canned	1 cup	28

Cereals, continued	Measure	Grams Carbohydrate
Spaghetti in tomato sauce		
with cheese, home recipe	1 cup	37
with cheese, canned	1 cup	38
Wheat, puffed	1 cup	12
Wheat flakes	¾ cup	18
Wheat, shredded, plain (long, round, or bite-size)	1 ounce (1 large biscuit or ½ cup bite-size)	20
Wheat flours		
whole wheat	1 cup stirred	85
all-purpose	1 cup sifted	88
buckwheat, light	1 cup	78
self-rising, enriched	1 cup	93
cake or pastry	1 cup sifted	76

Desserts

Brownies, with nuts		
homemade	1	10
made from a mix	1	13
Cakes		
angel food cake	2½-inch piece (one twelfth of 9¾-inch round cake)	32
butter cake, plain, without icing	1¾-inch piece (one sixteenth of 9-inch round cake)	32
	1 cupcake about 2¾ inches in diameter	14

Desserts, continued	Measure	Grams Carbohydrate
butter cake, plain, with chocolate icing	1¾-inch piece (one sixteenth of 9-inch round layer cake)	45
	1 cupcake about 2¾ inches in diameter	21
chocolate, with chocolate icing	1¾-inch piece (one sixteenth of 9-inch round layer cake)	40
	1 cupcake about 2¾ inches in diameter	20
fruitcake, dark	one thirtieth of 8-inch loaf	9
gingerbread	1 piece about 2¾ x 2¾ x 1⅜ inches	32
pound cake, old-fashioned	1 slice about 3½ x 3 x ½ inches	14
sponge cake	one twelfth of 10-inch round cake	36

Cookies

chocolate chip, home-made	1, about 2½ inches in diameter	16
chocolate chip, commercial	1	7
fig bars	1 small	11
sandwich, chocolate or vanilla	1, about 1¾ inches in diameter	7
Custard, baked	1 cup	29
Gelatin desserts, plain	½ cup	17

Ice cream

regular (about 10 percent fat)	1 cup	28
rich (about 16 percent fat)	1 cup	27

Desserts, continued	Measure	Grams Carbohydrate
Ice milk		
hardened	1 cup	29
soft serve	1 cup	39
Pies		
apple	one eighth of 9-inch pie	51
butterscotch	one eighth of 9-inch pie	50
Boston cream pie	one twelfth of 8-inch round cake	34
cherry	one eighth of 9-inch pie	52
custard, plain	one eighth of 9-inch pie	30
lemon meringue	one eighth of 9-inch pie	45
mince	one eighth of 9-inch pie	56
pecan	one eighth of 9-inch pie	60
pineapple chiffon	one eighth of 9-inch pie	36
pumpkin	one eighth of 9-inch pie	32
Piecrust—baked shell made with enriched flour	1 shell	79
Piecrust—made from packaged mix	crust for double-crust pie	141
Puddings		
cornstarch, vanilla	1 cup	41
cornstarch, chocolate	1 cup	67

Desserts, continued	Measure	Grams Carbohydrate
chocolate, from a mix	½ cup	26
tapioca cream	½ cup	14
Sherbet	1 cup	59

Fats, Oils, and Related Products

Butter or margarine	1 tablespoon	trace
	1 pat 1 inch square ¼ inch thick	trace
Margarine, whipped	1 tablespoon	trace
	1 pat 1¼ inches square, ¼ inch thick	trace
Cooking fats		
vegetable	1 tablespoon	0
lard	1 tablespoon	0
Salad or cooking oils	1 tablespoon	0
Salad dressings, regular		
blue cheese	1 tablespoon	1
French	1 tablespoon	3
home-cooked, boiled	1 tablespoon	2
mayonnaise	1 tablespoon	trace
mayonnaise-type, commercial, plain	1 tablespoon	2
thousand island	1 tablespoon	3
Salad dressings, low calorie		
French	1 tablespoon	trace
mayonnaise-type	1 tablespoon	1

Soups

	Measure	Grams Carbohydrate
Bean with pork	1 cup	22
Beef noodle	1 cup	7
Bouillon, broth, and con- somme	1 cup	3
Clam chowder		
Manhattan	1 cup	12
New England	1 cup	16
Cream of chicken		
with water	1 cup	8
with milk	1 cup	15
Cream of mushroom		
with water	1 cup	10
with milk	1 cup	16
Cream of potato		
with water	1 cup	12
with milk	1 cup	18
Cream of shrimp		
with water	1 cup	8
with milk	1 cup	15
Dehydrated soups		
chicken noodle	2-ounce package	33
onion	1½-ounce package	23
tomato vegetable with noodles	2½-ounce package	45
Minestrone	1 cup	14
Oyster stew (frozen)		
with water	1 cup	8
with milk	1 cup	14
Split pea	1 cup	21

Soups, continued	Measure	Grams Carbohydrate
Tomato		
with water	1 cup	16
with milk	1 cup	23
Vegetable beef	1 cup	10
Vegetarian vegetable	1 cup	13

Sugars, Sweets, and Related Products

Caramels	1 ounce (3 medium caramels)	22
Milk chocolate, sweetened	1-ounce bar	16
Chocolate-coated peanuts	1 ounce	11
Candy corn	1 ounce (20 pieces)	25
Mints	1 ounce (3 mints about 1½ inches in diameter)	25
Fudge, vanilla or chocolate, plain	1 ounce	21
Gumdrops	1 ounce (2 to 3 large or about 20 small)	25
Hard candy	1 ounce (3 to 4 candy balls about ¾ inch in diameter)	28
Marshmallows	1 ounce (4 marshmallows—63 to a pound)	23
Chocolate syrup		
thin type	1 fluid ounce	24
fudge type	1 fluid ounce	20
Honey, strained or extracted	1 tablespoon	17

Sweets, continued	Measure	Grams Carbohydrate
Molasses		
cane, light	1 tablespoon	13
blackstrap	1 tablespoon	11
Syrup, table blends	1 tablespoon	15
Jams, preserves	1 tablespoon	14
Jellies, marmalades	1 tablespoon	13
Sugar		
white, granulated	1 tablespoon	11
brown, packed	1 tablespoon	13

Beverages

	Measure	Grams Carbohydrate
Alcoholic beverages		
beer, 3.6 percent alcohol by weight	12 ounces	14
gin, rum, whisky, vodka		
100-proof	1½ ounces	trace
90-proof	1½ ounces	trace
86-proof	1½ ounces	trace
80-proof	1½ ounces	trace
table wines (such as Chablis, claret, Rhine wine, sauterne)	3½ ounces	4
dessert wines (such as muscatel, port, sherry, Tokay)	3½ ounces	8
Carbonated beverages		
carbonated water	12 ounces	29
ginger ale	12 ounces	29
cola-type	12 ounces	37
fruit-flavored soda (10 to 13 percent sugar)	12 ounces	45

Beverages, continued	Measure	Grams Carbohydrate
root beer	12 ounces	45
Tom Collins mix	12 ounces	45
Fruit drinks		
cranberry juice cocktail, canned	½ cup	21
grape juice drink	1 cup	35
lemonade, frozen concentrate, diluted, ready-to-serve	½ cup	14
limeade, frozen concentrate, diluted, ready-to-serve	1 cup	27
orange-apricot juice drink	½ cup	16
orange-grapefruit juice drink	½ cup	13
Fruit juices		
apple juice, canned	½ cup	15
grape juice, bottled	½ cup	21
grape juice, frozen concentrate, diluted, ready-to-serve	1 cup	33
grapefruit juice		
fresh	1 cup	23
canned, unsweetened	1 cup	24
canned, sweetened	1 cup	32
frozen concentrate, diluted, ready-to-serve, unsweetened	1 cup	24
made from dehydrated crystals and water	1 cup	24

Beverages, continued	Measure	Grams Carbohydrate
lemon juice, fresh or canned	4 tablespoons	5
lime juice, fresh or canned	½ cup	11
orange juice		
fresh	½ cup	13
canned, unsweetened	½ cup	14
frozen concentrate, diluted, ready-to-serve	1 cup	29
made from dehydrated crystals and water	1 cup	27
pineapple juice, canned, unsweetened	½ cup	17
prune juice, canned	1 cup	49
tangerine juice, canned, sweetened	½ cup	15

Milk beverages

cocoa, homemade	1 cup	27
chocolate-flavored drink made with skim milk	1 cup	27
malted milk	1 cup	28

Snacks and Extras

Barbecue sauce	¼ cup	5
Bouillon cube	½-inch cube	trace
Olives, green	4 medium, 3 large, or 2 giant	trace
Olives, ripe	3 small or 2 large	trace

Snacks, continued	Measure	Grams Carbohydrate
Pickles, cucumber		
dill	1, about 4 inches long, 1¼ inches in diameter	1
sweet	1, about 2½ inches long, ¾ inch in diameter	6
fresh	2 slices 1½ inches in diameter	3
Popcorn, popped (with oil and salt added)	1 cup large kernels	5
Potato chips	10, about 1¾ x 2½ inches	10
Pretzels, Dutch, twisted	1	12
Pretzels, stick	5 regular (3⅛ inches long) or 10 small (2¼ inches long)	2
Relish, finely chopped, sweet	1 tablespoon	5
Tomato catsup	1 tablespoon	4
Tartare sauce	2 tablespoons	2
White sauce, medium (made with 1 cup milk to 2 tablespoons fat and 2 tablespoons flour)	½ cup	11
Vinegar	1 tablespoon	1
Doughnuts, cake-type, plain	1, about 3¼ inches in diameter	16
French fries		
fresh, cooked in deep fat	10, about 2 inches long	20
frozen, heated, ready-to-serve	10, about 2 inches long	19

Snacks, continued	Measure	Grams Carbohydrate
Hamburger	2-ounce meat patty, with roll	21
Hot dog	1 average, with roll	21

Miscellaneous

Artichokes, globe or French, boiled	1	15
Bamboo shoots, raw	1 pound or approximately 3 cups of 1-inch pieces	24
Caviar, sturgeon, granular or pressed	1 tablespoon	1
Limburger cheese	1 ounce	1
Chestnuts	10 nuts	31
Chewing gum, candy-coated	1 piece	2
Chop suey, with meat, no noodles, made from home recipe	1 cup	13
Chow mein, chicken, no noodles, made from home recipe	1 cup	10
Chow mein, canned	1 cup	18
Herring		
in tomato sauce	1 herring with 1 tablespoon sauce	2
pickled	1 herring	0
smoked, kippered, drained	1 7-inch fillet	0
Lobster Newburg	1 cup	13
Loquats, raw	10	15
Lychees, raw	10	15

Miscellaneous, continued	Measure	Grams Carbohydrate
Mangoes, raw	1	39
Pâté de foie gras, canned	1 tablespoon	1
Persimmons		
Japanese or kaki	1	33
native	1	8
Pigs' feet, pickled	2 ounces	0
Pine nuts		
pignolias	1 ounce	3
piñon	1 ounce	6
Plantains (baking bananas), raw	1	82
Rabbit, domesticated, flesh only, stewed	1 cup	0
Sunflower seed kernels, dry	¼ cup	14
Welsh rarebit	1 cup	15

Calories—
Metric Portions

Milk and Milk Products

	Measure	Calories
Milk		
whole	237 milliliters	160
skim	237 milliliters	90
partly skimmed (2 percent), nonfat milk solids added	237 milliliters	145
buttermilk	237 milliliters	90
evaporated milk, undiluted	118 milliliters	175
condensed milk, sweetened, undiluted	118 milliliters	490
Cream		
half-and-half (milk and cream)	15 milliliters	20
light, coffee or table	15 milliliters	30
sour cream	15 milliliters	25
whipped topping (pressurized)	15 milliliters	10
whipping cream, unwhipped (volume about double when whipped), light	15 milliliters	45
whipping cream, unwhipped, heavy	15 milliliters	55

Milk, continued	Measure	Calories
Imitation cream products (made with vegetable fat)		
creamer, powdered	5 milliliters	10
creamer, liquid (frozen)	15 milliliters	20
sour dressing (imitation sour cream) made with nonfat dry milk	15 milliliters	20
whipped topping, pressurized	15 milliliters	10
whipped topping, frozen	15 milliliters	10
whipped topping, powdered, made with whole milk	15 milliliters	10
Cheese		
natural cheeses		
blue or Roquefort type	28 grams	105
	2½-centimeter cube	65
Camembert, packed in 113-gram package, three wedges per package	1 wedge	115
cheddar	28 grams	115
	2½-centimeter cube	70
	57 grams grated	225
Parmesan, grated	15 milliliters	25
	28 grams	130
Swiss	28 grams	105
	2½-centimeter cube	55
pasteurized processed cheeses		
American	28 grams	105
	2½-centimeter cube	65
Swiss	28 grams	100
	2½-centimeter cube	65

Milk, continued	Measure	Calories
American cheese food	15 milliliters	45
	2½-centimeter cube	55
American cheese spread	15 milliliters	40
	28 grams	80
cottage cheese, large or small curd		
creamed	227 grams, curd packed	260
	28 grams	30
uncreamed	227 grams, curd packed	170
	28 grams	20
cream cheese	28 grams	105
	2½-centimeter cube	60

Yogurt

made from partially skimmed milk	237 milliliters	125
made from whole milk	237 milliliters	150

Meat

Beef

pot roast, braised or simmered, lean and fat	85 grams (1 thick or 2 thin slices about 10 x 5½ centimeters)	245
pot roast, braised or simmered, lean only	85 grams (1 thick or 2 thin slices about 10 x 5½ centimeters)	165
oven roast cut relatively fat, such as rib; lean and fat	85 grams (1 thick or 2 thin slices about 10 x 5¾ centimeters)	375

Meat, continued	Measure	Calories
oven roast cut relatively fat, lean only	85 grams (1 thick or 2 thin slices about 10 x 5¾ centimeters)	205
oven roast cut relatively lean, such as round; lean and fat	85 grams (1 thick or 2 thin slices about 10 x 5¾ centimeters)	220
oven roast cut relatively lean; lean only	85 grams (1 thick or 2 thin slices about 10 x 5¾ centimeters)	160
steak, broiled, cut relatively fat, such as sirloin; lean and fat	85 grams (1 piece about 9 x 5 x 2 centimeters)	330
steak, broiled, cut relatively fat; lean only	85 grams (1 piece about 9 x 5 x 2 centimeters)	175
steak, broiled, cut relatively lean, such as round; lean and fat	85 grams (1 piece about 10 x 5 x 1¼ centimeters)	220
steak, broiled, cut relatively lean; lean only	85 grams (1 piece about 10 x 5 x 1¼ centimeters)	160
hamburger patty, broiled, panbroiled, or sautéed	85-gram patty (about 6½ centimeters in diameter, 2 centimeters thick)	245
lean ground beef	85-gram patty (about 6½ centimeters in diameter, 2 centimeters thick)	185

Meat, continued	**Measure**	**Calories**
corned beef, canned	85 grams (1 piece about 10 x 6 x 1¼ centimeters)	185
corned beef hash, canned	85 grams	155
dried beef, chipped	57 grams	115
dried beef, creamed	118 milliliters	190
beef and vegetable stew, canned	237 milliliters	195
beef and vegetable stew, homemade, with lean beef	237 milliliters	220
beef pot pie, homemade	one fourth of pie 23 centimeters in diameter	385
chili con carne, canned, without beans	237 milliliters	480
chili con carne, canned, with beans	237 milliliters	340

Veal

cutlet, broiled, trimmed, meat only	85 grams (1 piece about 9½ x 6 x 1 centimeters)	185
roast, cooked, without bone	85 grams (1 thick or 2 thin slices about 10 x 5¾ centimeters)	230

Lamb

loin chop (about seven chops to a kilogram, as purchased), lean and fat	99 grams	355
loin chop, lean only	66 grams	120

Meat, continued	Measure	Calories
loin chop, broiled without bone; lean and fat	85 grams	305
loin chop, broiled without bone; lean only	85 grams	160
leg of lamb, roasted, lean and fat	85 grams (1 thick or 2 thin slices about 10 x 5¾ centimeters)	235
leg of lamb, lean only	85 grams (1 thick or 2 thin slices about 10 x 5¾ centimeters)	175

Pork, fresh

chop (about seven chops to a kilogram, as purchased), lean and fat	76 grams	305
chop, lean only	57 grams	150
roast, loin, lean and fat	85 grams (1 thick or 2 thin slices about 9 x 6 centimeters)	310
roast, loin, lean only	85 grams (1 thick or 2 thin slices about 9 x 6 centimeters)	215

Pork, cured

ham, cooked, lean and fat	85 grams (1 thick or 2 thin slices about 9 x 6 centimeters)	245
ham, cooked, lean only	85 grams (1 thick or 2 thin slices about 9 x 6 centimeters)	160

Meat, continued	Measure	Calories
bacon, broiled or fried crisp	2 thin slices (62 slices per kilogram)	60
	2 medium slices (44 slices per kilogram)	85
bacon, Canadian, cooked	1 slice about 8½ centimeters in diameter, ½ centimeter thick	60

Sausage and variety and luncheon meats

bologna	57 grams (2 very thin slices about 11½ centimeters in diameter)	170
braunschweiger	57 grams (2 slices about 8 centimeters in diameter)	180
Vienna sausage, canned	57 grams	135
pork sausage, link	4 links 10 centimeters long (113 grams, uncooked)	250
pork sausage, bulk	2 patties about 10 centimeters in diameter, ⅔ centimeter thick (113 grams, uncooked)	260
beef liver, fried (including fat for frying)	85 grams (1 piece about 16½ x 6 x 1 centimeters)	195
beef heart, braised, trimmed of fat	85 grams (1 thick piece about 10 x 6 centimeters)	160
salami	57 grams (2 slices about 11½ centimeters in diameter)	175

Meat, continued	Measure	Calories
beef tongue, braised	85 grams (1 slice about 7½ x 5 x 1 centimeters)	210
frankfurter	57-gram frankfurter	170
boiled ham (luncheon meat)	57 grams (2 very thin slices about 16 x 10 centimeters)	135
spiced ham, canned	57 grams (2 thin slices about 7½ x 5 centimeters)	165

Poultry

Chicken

broiled (no skin)	85 grams (about one fourth of a broiler)	115
fried	one half breast 79 grams, meat only	120
	1 drumstick, 38 grams, meat only	90
canned, meat only	99 grams (118 milliliters)	200
Poultry pie, homemade	one fourth of pie 23 centimeters in diameter	410

Turkey

roasted, light meat (no skin)	85 grams (1 thick or 2 thin slices about 11 x 5 centimeters)	150
roasted, dark meat (no skin)	85 grams (1 thick or 2 thin slices about 11 x 5 centimeters)	175

Fish and Shellfish

	Measure	Calories
Bluefish, baked with fat	85 grams (1 piece about 9 x 5 x 1¼ centimeters)	135
Clams, shelled, raw, meat only	85 grams (about 4 medium clams)	65
Clams, canned, clams and juice	85 grams (about 118 milliliters—3 medium clams and juice)	45
Crabmeat, canned or cooked	85 grams (118 milliliters)	80
Fish sticks (frozen), breaded, cooked (including breading and fat for frying)	85 grams (3 fish sticks 10 x 2½ x 1¼ centimeters)	150
Haddock, breaded, fried (including fat for frying)	85 grams (1 fillet about 10 x 6 x 1¼ centimeters)	140
Mackerel, broiled with fat	85 grams (1 piece about 10 x 7½ x 1¼ centimeters)	200
Mackerel, canned	85 grams, solids and liquids	155
Ocean perch, breaded, fried (including fat for frying)	85 grams (1 piece about 10 x 6 x 1¼ centimeters)	195
Oysters, raw, meat only	118 milliliters (6 to 10 medium-sized)	80
	85 grams	155
Salmon, broiled or baked	113 grams (1 steak about 11½ x 6 x 1¼ centimeters)	205

Fish, continued	Measure	Calories
Salmon, canned (pink)	85 grams, solids and liquids	120
Sardines, canned in oil	85 grams, drained solids (7 medium sardines)	170
Shrimp, canned, meat only	85 grams (27 medium shrimp)	100
Tunafish, canned in oil	85 grams, drained solids (59 milliliters)	170

Eggs

	Measure	Calories
Fried (including fat for frying)	1 large egg	100
Hard- or soft-boiled	1 large egg	80
Scrambled or omelet (including milk and fat for cooking)	1 large egg	110
Poached	1 large egg	80

Dry Beans and Peas

	Measure	Calories
Red kidney beans, canned or cooked	118 milliliters, solids and liquids	110
Lima beans, cooked	118 milliliters	130
Baked beans, canned, with pork and tomato sauce	118 milliliters	155
Baked beans, canned, with pork and sweet sauce	118 milliliters	190

Nuts

	Measure	Calories
Almonds	30 milliliters (15 almonds)	105

Nuts, continued	Measure	Calories
Brazil nuts	30 milliliters (4 to 5 large kernels)	115
Cashew nuts, roasted	30 milliliters (11 to 12 medium nuts)	100
Coconut, fresh, shredded meat	60 milliliters	110
Peanuts, roasted	60 milliliters	210
Peanut butter	15 milliliters	95
Pecan halves	30 milliliters (10 jumbo or 15 large)	95
Walnuts		
black or native, chopped	60 milliliters	200
English or Persian, halves	30 milliliters (6 to 7 halves)	80

Vegetables

Asparagus, cooked or canned	6 medium spears or 118 milliliters cut spears	20
Beans		
lima, cooked or canned	118 milliliters	90
snap—green, wax, or yellow—cooked or canned	118 milliliters	15
Beets, cooked or canned	118 milliliters diced, sliced, or small whole	30
Beet greens, cooked	118 milliliters	15

Vegetables, continued	Measure	Calories
Broccoli, cooked	118 milliliters chopped or 3 stalks 11½ to 12¾ centimeters long	25
Brussels sprouts, cooked	118 milliliters (4 sprouts 3 to 4 centimeters in diameter)	25

Cabbage

raw	118 milliliters shredded chopped, or sliced	10
coleslaw with mayonnaise	118 milliliters	85
coleslaw, with mayonnaise-type salad dressing	118 milliliters	60
cooked	118 milliliters	15

Carrots

raw	1, about 19 centimeters long, 3 centimeters in diameter	30
	118 milliliters, grated	25
cooked or canned	118 milliliters	25
Cauliflower, cooked	237 milliliters	30

Celery

raw	3 inner stalks about 12¾ centimeters long	10
cooked	118 milliliters diced	10
Chard, cooked	118 milliliters	15
Chicory, raw	118 milliliters	5
Chives, raw	15 milliliters	trace
Collards, cooked	118 milliliters	25

Vegetables, continued	Measure	Calories
Corn		
on the cob, cooked	1 ear about 12¾ centimeters long, 4½ centimeters in diameter	70
kernels, cooked or canned	118 milliliters	70
cream-style	118 milliliters	105
Cress, garden, cooked	118 milliliters	15
Cucumber, raw, pared	6 center slices 3 millimeters thick	5
Dandelion greens, cooked	118 milliliters	15
Eggplant, cooked	118 milliliters	20
Endive, raw	118 milliliters	5
Kale, cooked	118 milliliters	20
Kohlrabi, cooked	118 milliliters	20
Lettuce, raw	2 large leaves	5
	118 milliliters shredded or chopped	5
	1 wedge—one sixth head	10
Mushrooms, canned	118 milliliters	20
Mustard greens, cooked	118 milliliters	15
Okra, cooked	118 milliliters cuts and pods	35
	118 milliliters sliced	25
Onions		
young, green, raw	2 medium or 6 small, without tops	15
	15 milliliters chopped	5
mature, raw	15 milliliters chopped	5
mature, cooked	118 milliliters	30
Parsley, raw	15 milliliters chopped	trace

Vegetables, continued	Measure	Calories
Parsnips, cooked	118 milliliters diced	50
	118 milliliters mashed	70
Peas, green, cooked or canned	118 milliliters	65
Peppers, green		
raw	1 ring 6 millimeters thick	trace
	15 milliliters chopped	trace
cooked	1 medium, about 7 centimeters long, 6 centimeters in diameter	15
Potatoes		
baked	1, about 12 centimeters long, 6 centimeters in diameter	145
boiled	1, about 6 centimeters in diameter	90
chips	10, about 4½ x 6 centimeters	115
French-fried, fresh, cooked in deep fat	10, 9 to 10 centimeters long	215
French-fried, frozen, heated, ready-to-serve	10, 9 to 10 centimeters long	170
pan fried from raw	118 milliliters	230
hash browned	118 milliliters	175
mashed, milk added	118 milliliters	70
mashed, milk and fat added	118 milliliters	100
mashed, made from granules, with milk and fat added	118 milliliters	100

Vegetables, continued	Measure	Calories
au gratin	118 milliliters	180
scalloped, without cheese	118 milliliters	125
salad, made with cooked salad dressing	118 milliliters	125
salad, made with mayonnaise or French dressing and eggs	118 milliliters	180
sticks	118 milliliters	95
Pumpkin, canned	118 milliliters	40
Radishes, raw	4 medium	4
Rutabagas, cooked	118 milliliters diced or sliced	30
Sauerkraut, canned	118 milliliters	20
Spinach, cooked or canned	118 milliliters	25
Squash		
summer, cooked	118 milliliters	15
winter, baked	118 milliliters mashed	65
winter, boiled	118 milliliters mashed	45
Sweet potatoes		
baked in skin	1, about 12¾ centimeters long, 5 centimeters in diameter	160
candied	one half about 6 centimeters long	160
canned	118 milliliters mashed	140
Tomatoes		
raw	1, about 6 centimeters in diameter	20
cooked or canned	118 milliliters	30
Tomato juice, canned	118 milliliters	25

Vegetables, continued	Measure	Calories
Tomato juice cocktail, canned	118 milliliters	25
Turnips		
raw	118 milliliters cubed or sliced	20
cooked	118 milliliters diced	20
Turnip greens, cooked	118 milliliters	15
Vegetable juice cocktail	118 milliliters	20
Watercress, raw	10 sprigs	5

Fruits

Apples, raw	1 medium (about 7 centimeters in diameter)	80
Apple juice, canned	118 milliliters	60
Applesauce		
sweetened	118 milliliters	115
unsweetened	118 milliliters	50
Apricots		
raw	3 (about 26 per kilogram as purchased)	55
canned, water pack	118 milliliters halves and liquid	45
canned, heavy syrup pack	118 milliliters halves and syrup	110
dried, cooked, unsweetened	118 milliliters fruit and juice	105
Avocados		
California varieties	one half of 284-gram avocado (about 8 centimeters in diameter)	190

Fruits, continued	Measure	Calories
Florida varieties	one half of 454-gram avocado (about 9¼ centimeters in diameter)	205
Bananas, raw	1 banana 15¼ to 17¾ centimeters long	85
	1 banana 20¼ to 23 centimeters long	100
Blackberries, raw	118 milliliters	40
Blueberries		
fresh, raw	118 milliliters	45
frozen, sweetened	118 milliliters	120
frozen, unsweetened	118 milliliters	45
Raspberries		
fresh, red, raw	118 milliliters	35
frozen, red, sweetened	118 milliliters	120
fresh, black, raw	118 milliliters	50
Strawberries		
fresh, raw	118 milliliters	30
frozen, sweetened	118 milliliters sliced	140
Cantaloupe, raw	one half of melon about 12¾ centimeters in diameter	80
Cherries		
sour, raw, with pits	118 milliliters	30
sour, canned (water pack), pitted	118 milliliters	50
sweet, raw, with pits	118 milliliters	40
sweet, canned (water pack), with pits	118 milliliters	65
sweet, canned (syrup pack), with pits	118 milliliters	105

Fruits, continued	Measure	Calories
Cranberry sauce, sweetened, canned	30 milliliters	50
Dates, fresh, dried, pitted, cut	118 milliliters	245

Figs

raw	3 small about 4 centimeters in diameter (about 113 grams)	95
canned, heavy syrup	118 milliliters	110
dried	1 large, about 5 x 2½ centimeters	60
Fruit cocktail, canned in heavy syrup	118 milliliters	95

Grapefruit

raw, white	one half medium (about 9½ centimeters in diameter)	45
raw, pink or red	one half medium (about 9½ centimeters in diameter)	50
canned, water pack	118 milliliters	35
canned, syrup pack	118 milliliters	90

Grapefruit juice

fresh	118 milliliters	50
canned, unsweetened	118 milliliters	50
canned, sweetened	118 milliliters	65
frozen concentrate, diluted, ready-to-serve, unsweetened	118 milliliters	50
frozen, concentrate, diluted, ready-to-serve, sweetened	118 milliliters	60

Fruits, continued	Measure	Calories
Grapes		
American type (Concord, Delaware, Niagara, Scuppernong), slip skin	1 bunch about 9 x 7½ centimeters (about 99 grams)	45
	118 milliliters	35
European type (Malaga, Muscat, Thompson seedless, Flame Tokay), adherent skin	118 milliliters	55
Grape juice		
bottled	118 milliliters	85
frozen concentrate, diluted, ready-to-serve	118 milliliters	65
Honeydew melon, raw	1 wedge about 5 x 17¾ centimeters	50
Lemon juice, fresh or canned	118 milliliters	30
	15 milliliters	5
Lemonade, frozen concentrate, diluted, ready-to-serve	118 milliliters	55
Oranges, raw	1, about 6¾ centimeters in diameter	65
Orange juice		
fresh	118 milliliters	55
canned, unsweetened	118 milliliters	60
frozen concentrate, diluted, ready-to-serve	118 milliliters	55
Peaches		
raw	1 medium (about 6 centimeters in diameter)	40
	118 milliliters sliced	30

Fruits, continued	Measure	Calories
canned, water pack	118 milliliters	40
canned, syrup pack	118 milliliters	100
dried, cooked, unsweetened	118 milliliters (5 to 6 halves and liquid)	100
frozen, sweetened	118 milliliters	110

Pears

raw	1, about 9 centimeters long, 6 centimeters in diameter	100
canned, water pack	118 milliliters	40
canned, syrup pack	118 milliliters	95

Pineapple

raw	118 milliliters diced	40
canned in heavy syrup —crushed, tidbits, or chunks	118 milliliters	95
canned in heavy syrup, sliced	2 small slices or 1 large and 30 milliliters juice	80

Pineapple juice, canned, unsweetened	118 milliliters	70

Plums

raw, Damson	5, about 2½ centimeters in diameter	30
raw, Japanese	1, about 5½ centimeters in diameter	30
canned (syrup pack), with pits	118 milliliters	105

Prunes, cooked

unsweetened	118 milliliters fruit and liquid	125
sweetened	118 milliliters fruit and liquid	205

Fruits, continued	Measure	Calories
Prune juice, canned	118 milliliters	100
Raisins	118 milliliters, packed	240
Rhubarb, cooked, sweetened	118 milliliters	190
Tangerines, raw	1 medium (about 6 centimeters in diameter)	40

Tangerine juice		
canned, unsweetened	118 milliliters	55
canned, sweetened	118 milliliters	60
Watermelon, raw	1 wedge about 10 x 20 centimeters	110

Breads

Cracked wheat bread	1 slice	65
Raisin bread	1 slice	65
Rye bread	1 slice	60

White bread		
soft crumb, regular slice	1 slice	70
soft crumb, thin slice	1 slice	55
firm crumb	1 slice	65

Whole-wheat bread		
soft crumb	1 slice	65
firm crumb	1 slice	60

Biscuits		
baking powder, home recipe	1, about 5 centimeters in diameter	105
baking powder, from a mix	1, about 5 centimeters in diameter	90

Breads, continued	Measure	Calories
Crackers		
butter	1, about 5 centimeters in diameter	15
cheese	1, about 5 centimeters in diameter	15
graham	4 small or 2 medium	55
saltine	4, about 5 centimeters square	50
matzoh	1, about 15 centimeters in diameter	80
pilot	1	75
oyster	10	35
rye	2, about 5 x 9 centimeters	45
Danish pastry, plain	1, about 11½ centimeters in diameter	275
Doughnuts		
cake-type, plain	1, about 8 centimeters in diameter	165
yeast-leavened, raised	1, about 9½ centimeters in diameter	175
Muffins		
plain	1, about 7½ centimeters in diameter	120
blueberry	1, about 6 centimeters in diameter	110
bran	1, about 6¾ centimeters in diameter	105
corn	1, about 6 centimeters in diameter	125
Pancakes		
wheat (home recipe or mix)	1, about 10 centimeters in diameter	60

Breads, continued	Measure	Calories
buckwheat (made with buckwheat pancake mix)	1, about 10 centimeters in diameter	55
Pizza (cheese)	13½-centimeter piece (one eighth of 35-centimeter pie)	155
Pretzels, Dutch, twisted	1	60
Pretzels, stick	5 regular (8 centimeters long) or 10 small (5¾ centimeters long)	10

Rolls

	Measure	Calories
hamburger or frankfurter	1 roll (35 per kilogram)	120
hard, round or rectangular	1 roll (20 per kilogram)	155
plain, pan	1 roll (35 per kilogram)	85
sweet, pan	1 roll (24 per kilogram)	135
Waffles	1, about 18 centimeters in diameter	210
Spoonbread	118 milliliters	235

Cereals and Other Grain Products

	Measure	Calories
Bran flakes (40 percent bran)	237 milliliters	106
Bran flakes with raisins	237 milliliters	135
Corn, puffed, presweetened	237 milliliters	115
Corn, shredded	237 milliliters	96
Corn flakes	237 milliliters	96

Cereals, continued	Measure	Calories
Corn flakes, sugar-coated	158 milliliters	110
Corn grits, degermed, cooked	178 milliliters	95
Farina, cooked (quick-cooking)	178 milliliters	80
Macaroni, cooked	178 milliliters	115
Macaroni and cheese		
homemade	118 milliliters	215
canned	118 milliliters	115
Noodles, cooked	178 milliliters	150
Oats, puffed	237 milliliters	99
Oats, puffed, sugar-coated	237 milliliters	144
Oatmeal or rolled oats, cooked	178 milliliters	100
Rice, "instant," ready-to-serve	178 milliliters	135
Rice flakes	237 milliliters	110
Rice, puffed	237 milliliters	57
Rice, puffed, presweetened	158 milliliters	110
Rice, shredded	237 milliliters	104
Spaghetti, cooked	178 milliliters	115
Spaghetti with meat balls		
home recipe	178 milliliters	250
canned	178 milliliters	195
Spaghetti in tomato sauce		
with cheese, home recipe	178 milliliters	195
with cheese, canned	178 milliliters	140
Wheat, puffed	237 milliliters	56
Wheat, puffed, presweetened	237 milliliters	131
Wheat, rolled, cooked	178 milliliters	135

Cereals, continued	Measure	Calories
Wheat, shredded, plain (long, round, or bite-size)	28.35 grams (1 large biscuit or 118 milliliters bite-size)	100
Wheat flakes	237 milliliters	100

Wheat flours

whole wheat	237 milliliters stirred	400
all-purpose	237 milliliters sifted	420
Wheat germ, toasted	15 milliliters	25

Desserts

Apple Betty	118 milliliters	160
Brownie, with nuts	1, about 4½ centimeters square, 2 centimeters thick	90

Cakes

angel food cake	6-centimeter piece (one twelfth of 25-centimeter round cake)	135
butter cake, plain, without icing	1 piece about 7½ x 7½ x 5 centimeters	315
	1 cupcake about 7 centimeters in diameter	115
butter cake, plain, with chocolate icing	4½-centimeter piece (one sixteenth of 23-centimeter round layer cake)	240
	1 cupcake about 7 centimeters in diameter	170

Desserts, continued	Measure	Calories
chocolate, with chocolate icing	4½-centimeter piece (one sixteenth of 23-centimeter round layer cake)	235
fruitcake, dark	1 piece about 5 x 4 centimeters	55
gingerbread	1 piece about 7 x 7 x 3½ centimeters	175
pound cake, old-fashioned	1 slice about 9 x 7½ x 1¼ centimeters	140
sponge cake	4¾-centimeter piece (one sixteenth of 25-centimeter round cake)	145

Cookies

chocolate chip	1, about 6 centimeters in diameter	50
fig bars	1 small	50
sandwich, chocolate or vanilla	1, about 4½ centimeters in diameter	50
sugar	1, about 5¾ centimeters in diameter	35
vanilla wafer	1, about 4½ centimeters in diameter	20
Custard, baked	118 milliliters	150
Fruit ice	118 milliliters	125

Gelatin desserts
(ready-to-serve)

plain	118 milliliters	70
fruit added	118 milliliters	80

Desserts, continued	Measure	Calories
Ice cream		
regular (about 10 percent fat)	118 milliliters	130
rich (about 16 percent fat)	118 milliliters	165
Ice milk		
hardened	118 milliliters	100
soft serve	118 milliliters	135
Pies		
apple	one eighth of 23-centimeter pie	300
blueberry	one eighth of 23-centimeter pie	285
Boston cream pie	5½-centimeter piece of 20-centimeter round cake	210
cherry	one eighth of 23-centimeter pie	310
chocolate meringue	one eighth of 23-centimeter pie	285
coconut custard	one eighth of 23-centimeter pie	270
custard, plain	one eighth of 23-centimeter pie	250
lemon meringue	one eighth of 23-centimeter pie	270
mince	one eighth of 23-centimeter pie	320
peach	one eighth of 23-centimeter pie	300
pecan	one eighth of 23-centimeter pie	430

Desserts, continued	Measure	Calories
pumpkin	one eighth of 23-centimeter pie	240
raisin	one eighth of 23-centimeter pie	320
rhubarb	one eighth of 23-centimeter pie	300
strawberry	one eighth of 23-centimeter pie	185
Prune whip	118 milliliters	70

Puddings

cornstarch, vanilla	118 milliliters	140
chocolate, from a mix	118 milliliters	160
bread pudding, with raisins	118 milliliters	250
rennet desserts, ready-to-serve	118 milliliters	115
tapioca cream	118 milliliters	110
Sherbet	118 milliliters	130

Fats, Oils, and Related Products

Butter or margarine	15 milliliters	100
	1 pat 2½ centimeters square, ¾ centimeter thick	35
Margarine, whipped	15 milliliters	70
	1 pat 3 centimeters square, ¾ centimeter thick	25

Cooking fats

vegetable	15 milliliters	110
lard	15 milliliters	115
Salad or cooking oils	15 milliliters	120

Fats, Oils, continued	Measure	Calories
Salad dressings, regular		
blue cheese	15 milliliters	75
French	15 milliliters	65
home-cooked, boiled	15 milliliters	25
Italian	15 milliliters	85
mayonnaise	15 milliliters	100
mayonnaise-type, commercial, plain	15 milliliters	65
Russian	15 milliliters	75
thousand island	15 milliliters	80
Salad dressings, low calorie		
French	15 milliliters	15
Italian	15 milliliters	10
thousand island	15 milliliters	25

Soups

Bean with pork	237 milliliters	170
Beef noodle	237 milliliters	65
Bouillon, broth, and consomme	237 milliliters	30
Chicken gumbo	237 milliliters	55
Chicken noodle	237 milliliters	60
Chicken with rice	237 milliliters	50
Clam chowder		
Manhattan	237 milliliters	80
New England	237 milliliters	135
Cream of asparagus		
with water	237 milliliters	65
with milk	237 milliliters	145

Soups, continued	Measure	Calories
Cream of chicken		
with water	237 milliliters	95
with milk	237 milliliters	180
Cream of mushroom		
with water	237 milliliters	135
with milk	237 milliliters	215
Minestrone	237 milliliters	105
Oyster stew (frozen)		
with water	237 milliliters	120
with milk	237 milliliters	200
Split pea	237 milliliters	145
Tomato		
with water	237 milliliters	90
with milk	237 milliliters	170
Vegetable with broth	237 milliliters	80

Sugars, Sweets, and Related Products

Caramels	28 grams (3 medium caramels)	115
Chocolate creams	28 grams (2 to 3 pieces—77 to a kilogram)	125
Milk chocolate, sweetened	28-gram bar	145
Milk chocolate, sweetened, with almonds	28-gram bar	150
Chocolate mints	28 grams (1 to 2 mints—44 to a kilogram)	115
Candy corn	28 grams (20 pieces)	105
Mints	28 grams (3 mints about 4 centimeters in diameter)	105

Sweets, continued	Measure	Calories
Fudge (vanilla or chocolate)		
plain	28 grams	115
with nuts	28 grams	120
Gumdrops	28 grams (2 to 3 large or about 20 small)	100
Hard candy	28 grams (3 to 4 candy balls about 2 centimeters in diameter)	110
Jelly beans	28 grams (10 beans)	105
Marshmallows	28 grams (4 marsh-mallows—139 to a kilogram)	90
Peanut brittle	28 grams (1 to 2 pieces about 6 x 3 x 1 centimeters)	120
Chocolate syrup		
thin type	15 milliliters	45
fudge type	15 milliliters	60
Honey, strained or ex-tracted	15 milliliters	65
Molasses, cane, light	15 milliliters	50
Syrup, table blends	15 milliliters	55
Jams, preserves	15 milliliters	55
Jellies, marmalades	15 milliliters	50
Sugar—white, granulated, or brown, packed	5 milliliters	15

Beverages

Alcoholic beverages		
beer, 3.6 percent alco-hol by weight	237 milliliters	100

Beverages, continued	Measure	Calories
gin, rum, whisky, vodka		
100-proof	44 milliliters	125
90-proof	44 milliliters	110
86-proof	44 milliliters	105
80-proof	44 milliliters	95
table wines (such as Chablis, claret, Rhine wine, sauterne)	94 milliliters	85
dessert wines (such as muscatel, port, sherry, Tokay)	94 milliliters	140

Carbonated beverages

ginger ale	355 milliliters	115
cola-type	355 milliliters	145
fruit-flavored soda (10 to 13 percent sugar)	355 milliliters	170
root beer	355 milliliters	150

Check labels of low-calorie soft drinks for number of calories they contain.

Fruit drinks

apricot nectar	118 milliliters	70
cranberry juice cocktail	118 milliliters	80
grape drink	118 milliliters	70
lemonade, frozen concentrate, diluted, ready-to-serve	118 milliliters	55
orange-apricot juice drink	118 milliliters	60
peach drink	118 milliliters	60
pear nectar	118 milliliters	65
pineapple-grapefruit juice drink	118 milliliters	70

Beverages, continued	Measure	Calories
pineapple-orange juice drink	118 milliliters	70

Fruit juices

apple juice, canned	118 milliliters	60
grape juice, bottled	118 milliliters	85
grape juice, frozen concentrate, diluted, ready-to-serve	118 milliliters	65
grapefruit juice		
fresh	118 milliliters	50
canned, unsweetened	118 milliliters	50
canned, sweetened	118 milliliters	65
frozen concentrate, diluted, ready-to-serve, unsweetened	118 milliliters	50
frozen concentrate, diluted, ready-to-serve, sweetened	118 milliliters	60
lemon juice, fresh or canned	15 milliliters	5
orange juice		
fresh	118 milliliters	55
canned, unsweetened	118 milliliters	60
frozen concentrate, diluted, ready-to-serve	118 milliliters	55
pineapple juice, canned, unsweetened	118 milliliters	70
prune juice, canned	118 milliliters	100
tangerine juice, canned, unsweetened	118 milliliters	55
tangerine juice, canned, sweetened	118 milliliters	60

Beverages, continued	Measure	Calories
Milk beverages		
chocolate milk, home-made	237 milliliters	240
cocoa, homemade	237 milliliters	245
chocolate-flavored drink made with skim milk	237 milliliters	190
chocolate-flavored drink	237 milliliters	215
malted milk	237 milliliters	245
chocolate milkshake	355 milliliters	515

Snacks and Extras

Bouillon cube	1¼-centimeter cube	5
Olives, green	5 small, 3 large, or 2 giant	15
Olives, ripe	3 small or 2 large	15
Pickles, cucumber		
dill	1, about 10 centimeters long, 4½ centimeters in diameter	15
sweet	1, about 6 centimeters long, 2 centimeters in diameter	20
Popcorn, popped (with oil and salt added)	237 milliliters large kernels	40
Potato chips	10, about 4½ x 6 centimeters	115
Pretzels, Dutch, twisted	1	60

Snacks, continued	Measure	Calories
Pretzels, stick	5 regular (8 centimeters long) or 10 small (5¾ centimeters long)	10
Chili sauce, tomato	15 milliliters	15
Tomato catsup	15 milliliters	15
Gravy	30 milliliters	35
White sauce, medium (made with 237 milliliters milk to 30 milliliters flour and 30 milliliters fat)	118 milliliters	200
Cheese sauce (medium white sauce, above, with 30 milliliters grated cheese per 237 milliliters of sauce)	118 milliliters	205
Corn chips	237 milliliters	230

Doughnuts

cake-type, plain	1, about 8 centimeters in diameter	165
yeast-leavened	1, about 9½ centimeters in diameter	175

French fries

fresh, cooked in deep fat	10, 9 to 10 centimeters long	215
frozen, heated, ready-to-serve	10, 9 to 10 centimeters long	170
Hamburger	57-gram meat patty, with roll	280
Hot dog	1 average, with roll	290

Miscellaneous

	Measure	Calories
Artichokes, globe or French, boiled	1	12 to 67 (depends upon whether fresh or stored)
Bamboo shoots, raw	454 grams or approximately 710 milliliters of 2½-centimeter pieces	122
Caviar, sturgeon		
granular	15 milliliters	42
pressed	15 milliliters	54
Limburger cheese	28 grams	98
Chestnuts	10	141
Chewing gum, candy-coated	1 piece	5
Chop suey, with meat, no noodles, made from home recipe	237 milliliters	300
Chow mein, chicken, no noodles, made from home recipe	237 milliliters	255
Chow mein, canned	237 milliliters	95
Herring		
in tomato sauce	1 herring with 15 milliliters sauce	97
pickled	1 herring	112
smoked, kippered, drained	1 18-centimeter fillet	137
Lobster Newburg	237 milliliters	485
Loquats, raw	10	59
Lychees, raw	10	58
Mangoes, raw	1	152
Pâté de foie gras, canned	15 milliliters	60

Miscellaneous, continued	Measure	Calories
Persimmons		
Japanese or kaki	1	129
native	1	31
Pigs' feet, pickled	57 grams	113
Pine nuts		
pignolias	28 grams	156
piñon	28 grams	180
Plantains (baking bananas), raw	1	313
Rabbit, domesticated, flesh only, stewed	237 milliliters	302
Sunflower seed kernels, dry	59 milliliters	203
Welsh rarebit	237 milliliters	415

Carbohydrates—
Metric Portions

Milk and Milk Products

	Measure	Grams Carbohydrate
Milk		
whole	237 milliliters	12
skim	237 milliliters	12
partly skimmed (2 percent) nonfat milk solids added	237 milliliters	15
buttermilk	237 milliliters	12
evaporated milk, undiluted	118 milliliters	12
condensed milk, sweetened, undiluted	118 milliliters	83
nonfat dry milk, instant; low-density (1⅓ cups needed to prepare one quart)	237 milliliters	35
nonfat dry milk, instant; high-density (⅞ cup needed to prepare one quart)	237 milliliters	54
Cream		
half-and-half (milk and cream)	15 milliliters	1
light, coffee or table	15 milliliters	1
sour cream	15 milliliters	1

Milk, continued	Measure	Grams Carbohydrate
whipped topping (pressurized)	15 milliliters	trace
whipping cream, unwhipped (volume about double when whipped, light	15 milliliters	1
whipping cream, unwhipped, heavy	15 milliliters	1
Imitation cream products (made with vegetable fat)		
creamer, powdered	5 milliliters	1
creamer, liquid (frozen)	15 milliliters	2
sour dressing (imitation sour cream) made with nonfat dry milk	15 milliliters	1
whipped topping, pressurized	15 milliliters	trace
whipped topping, frozen	15 milliliters	1
whipped topping, powdered, made with whole milk	15 milliliters	1
Cheese		
natural cheeses		
blue or Roquefort type	28 grams	1
	2½-centimeter cube	trace
Camembert, packed in 113-gram package, three wedges per package	1 wedge	1
cheddar	28 grams	1
	2½-centimeter cube	trace
	57 grams grated	2

Milk, continued

	Measure	Grams Carbohydrate
Parmesan, grated	15 milliliters	trace
	28 grams	1
Swiss	28 grams	1
	2½-centimeter cube	trace
pasteurized processed cheeses		
American	28 grams	1
	2½-centimeter cube	trace
Swiss	28 grams	1
	2½-centimeter cube	trace
American cheese food	15 milliliters	1
	2½-centimeter cube	1
American cheese spread	28 grams	2
cottage cheese, large or small curd		
creamed	227 grams, curd packed	7
uncreamed	227 grams, curd packed	6
cream cheese	1 227-gram package	5
	2½-centimeter cube	trace

Yogurt

	Measure	Grams Carbohydrate
made from partially skimmed milk	237 milliliters	13
made from whole milk	237 milliliters	12

Meat

Beef

	Measure	Grams Carbohydrate
pot roast, braised or simmered, lean and fat	85 grams (1 thick or 2 thin slices about 10 x 5½ centimeters)	0

Meat, continued	Measure	Grams Carbohydrate
pot roast, braised or simmered, lean only	85 grams (1 thick or 2 thin slices about 10 x 5½ centimeters)	0
oven roast cut relatively fat, such as rib; lean and fat	85 grams (1 thick or 2 thin slices about 10 x 5¾ centimeters)	0
oven roast cut relatively fat; lean only	85 grams (1 thick or 2 thin slices about 10 x 5¾ centimeters)	0
oven roast cut relatively lean, such as round; lean and fat	85 grams (1 thick or 2 thin slices about 10 x 5¾ centimeters)	0
oven roast cut relatively lean; lean only	85 grams (1 thick or 2 thin slices about 10 x 5¾ centimeters)	0
steak, broiled, cut relatively fat, such as sirloin; lean and fat	85 grams (1 piece about 9 x 5 x 2 centimeters)	0
steak, broiled, cut relatively fat; lean only	85 grams (1 piece about 9 x 5 x 2 centimeters)	0
steak, broiled, cut relatively lean, such as round; lean and fat	85 grams (1 piece about 10 x 5 x 1¼ centimeters)	0
steak, broiled, cut relatively lean; lean only	85 grams (1 piece about 10 x 5 x 1¼ centimeters)	0

Meat, continued	**Measure**	**Grams Carbohydrate**
hamburger patty, broiled, panbroiled, or sautéed	85-gram patty (about 6½ centimeters in diameter, 2 centimeters thick)	0
lean ground beef	85-gram patty (about 6½ centimeters in diameter, 2 centimeters thick)	0
corned beef, canned	85 grams (1 piece about 10 x 6 x 1¼ centimeters)	0
corned beef hash, canned	85 grams	9
dried beef, chipped	57 grams	0
beef and vegetable stew, canned	237 milliliters	15
beef and vegetable stew, homemade, with lean beef	237 milliliters	15
beef pot pie	1 (11 centimeters in diameter)	43
chili con carne, canned, without beans	237 milliliters	15
chili con carne, canned, with beans	237 milliliters	30

Veal

cutlet, broiled, trimmed, meat only	85 grams (1 piece about 9½ x 6 x 1 centimeters)	0
roast, cooked, without bone	85 grams (1 thick or 2 thin slices about 10 x 5¾ centimeters)	0

Meat, continued	Measure	Grams Carbohydrate
Lamb		
loin chop (about seven chops to a kilogram, as purchased), lean and fat	99 grams	0
loin chop, lean only	66 grams	0
leg of lamb, roasted, lean and fat	85 grams (1 thick or 2 thin slices about 10 x 5¾ centimeters)	0
leg of lamb, lean only	85 grams (1 thick or 2 thin slices about 10 x 5¾ centimeters)	0
Pork, fresh		
chop (about seven chops to a kilogram, as purchased), lean and fat	76 grams	0
chop, lean only	57 grams	0
roast, loin, lean and fat	85 grams (1 thick or 2 thin slices about 9 x 6 centimeters)	0
roast, loin, lean only	85 grams (1 thick or 2 thin slices about 9 x 6 centimeters)	0
Pork, cured		
ham, cooked, lean and fat	85 grams (1 thick or 2 thin slices about 9 x 6 centimeters)	0
ham, cooked, lean only	85 grams (1 thick or 2 thin slices about 9 x 6 centimeters)	0

Meat, continued	Measure	Grams Carbohydrate
bacon, broiled or fried crisp	2 medium slices (44 slices per kilogram)	1

Sausage and variety and luncheon meats

bologna	57 grams (2 very thin slices about 11½ centimeters in diameter)	trace
braunschweiger	57 grams (2 slices about 8 centimeters in diameter)	1
Vienna sausage, canned	57 grams	1
pork sausage, link	4 links 10 centimeters long (113 grams, uncooked)	trace
pork sausage, bulk	2 patties about 10 centimeters in diameter, ⅔ centimeter thick (113 grams, uncooked)	trace
beef liver, fried (including fat for frying)	85 grams (1 piece about 16½ x 6 x 1 centimeters)	4
beef heart, braised, trimmed of fat	85 grams (1 thick piece about 10 x 6 centimeters)	1
salami	57 grams (2 slices about 11½ centimeters in diameter)	trace
frankfurter	57-gram frankfurter	0

Meat, continued	Measure	Grams Carbohydrate
boiled ham (luncheon meat)	57 grams (2 very thin slices about 16 x 10 centimeters)	0
spiced ham, canned	57 grams (2 thin slices about 7½ x 5 centimeters)	1
deviled ham, canned	15 milliliters	trace

Poultry

Chicken

broiled (no skin)	85 grams (about one fourth of a broiler)	0
fried	one half breast, 79 grams, meat only	1
	1 drumstick, 38 grams, meat only	trace
canned, meat only	99 grams (118 milliliters)	0
pot pie	1 (11 centimeters in diameter)	42

Turkey

roasted, light meat (no skin)	85 grams (1 thick or 2 thin slices about 11 x 5 centimeters)	0
roasted, dark meat (no skin)	85 grams (1 thick or 2 thin slices about 11 x 5 centimeters)	0

Fish and Shellfish

	Measure	Grams Carbohydrate
Bluefish, baked with fat	85 grams (1 piece about 9 x 5 x 1¼ centimeters	2
Clams, shelled, raw, meat only	85 grams (about 4 medium clams)	2
Clams, canned, clams and juice	85 grams (about 118 milliliters—3 medium clams and juice)	2
Crabmeat, canned or cooked	85 grams (118 milliliters)	1
Fish sticks (frozen), breaded, cooked (including breading and fat for frying)	85 grams (3 fish sticks 10 x 2½ x 1¼ centimeters)	5
Haddock, breaded, fried (including fat for frying)	85 grams (1 fillet about 10 x 6 x 1¼ centimeters)	5
Ocean perch, breaded, fried (including fat for frying)	85 grams (1 piece about 10 x 6 x 1¼ centimeters)	6
Oysters, raw, meat only	118 milliliters (6 to 10 medium-sized)	4
Salmon, canned (pink)	85 grams, solids and liquids	0
Sardines, canned in oil	85 grams, drained solids (7 medium sardines)	0
Shad, baked with fat and bacon	85 grams	0

Fish, continued	Measure	Grams Carbohydrate
Shrimp, canned, meat only	85 grams (27 medium shrimp)	1
Swordfish, broiled with fat	85 grams	0
Tunafish, canned in oil	85 grams, drained solids (59 milliliters)	0

Eggs

Fried (including fat for frying)	1 large egg	1
Hard- or soft-boiled	1 large egg	trace
Egg white	1	trace
Egg yolk	1	trace
Scrambled or omelet (including milk and fat for cooking)	1 large egg	1
Poached	1 large egg	trace

Dry Beans and Peas

Great Northern beans, cooked	237 milliliters	38
Navy (pea) beans, cooked	237 milliliters	40
Cowpeas or black-eyed peas, cooked	237 milliliters	34
Split peas, cooked	237 milliliters	52
Red kidney beans, canned or cooked	118 milliliters, solids and liquids	21
Lima beans, cooked	118 milliliters	25
Baked beans, canned, with pork and tomato sauce	118 milliliters	25

Dry Beans, continued	Measure	Grams Carbohydrate
Baked beans, canned, with pork and sweet sauce	118 milliliters	27

Nuts

Almonds	30 milliliters (15 almonds)	4
Cashew nuts, roasted	30 milliliters (11 to 12 medium nuts)	5
Coconut, fresh, shredded meat	60 milliliters	12
Peanuts, roasted	60 milliliters	7
Peanut butter	15 milliliters	3
Pecan halves	30 milliliters (10 jumbo or 15 large)	2
Walnuts, black or native, chopped	60 milliliters	5

Vegetables

Asparagus, cooked or canned	6 medium spears or 118 milliliters cut spears	3
Beans		
lima, cooked or canned	118 milliliters	17
snap—green, wax, or yellow—cooked	237 milliliters	7
snap—green, wax, or yellow—canned	237 milliliters	10
Beets		
cooked	118 milliliters	6
canned	118 milliliters	10

Vegetables, continued	Measure	Grams Carbohydrate
Beet greens, cooked	237 milliliters	5
Broccoli, cooked	118 milliliters chopped	4
	1 stalk 11½ to 12¾ centimeters long	8
Brussels sprouts, cooked	118 milliliters (4 sprouts, 3 to 4 centimeters in diameter)	5

Cabbage

raw	118 milliliters shredded, chopped, or sliced	4
cooked	118 milliliters	3
red cabbage, raw	237 milliliters coarsely shredded	5
Savoy cabbage, raw	237 milliliters coarsely shredded	3
Chinese cabbage, raw	237 milliliters of 2½-centimeter pieces	2

Carrots

raw	1, about 19 centimeters long, 3 centimeters in diameter	6
	118 milliliters, grated	6
cooked	118 milliliters	5
Cauliflower, cooked	237 milliliters	5

Celery

raw	3 inner stalks about 12¾ centimeters long	4
cooked	118 milliliters, diced	2
Collards, cooked	237 milliliters	9

Vegetables, continued	Measure	Grams Carbohydrate
Corn		
on the cob, cooked	1 ear about 12¾ centimeters long, 4½ centimeters in diameter	16
kernels, cooked or canned	118 milliliters	20
Cucumbers, raw, pared	6 center slices 3 millimeters thick	2
Dandelion greens, cooked	118 milliliters	6
Endive, raw	118 milliliters	2
Kale, cooked	118 milliliters	2
Lettuce		
raw, iceberg	1 wedge—one sixth head	2
loose-leaf types (such as romaine)	2 large leaves	2
butter-head types (such as Boston)	1 10-centimeter head	6
Mushrooms, canned	118 millilters	3
Mustard greens, cooked	118 milliliters	3
Okra, cooked	8 pods	5
Onions		
young, green, raw	2 medium or 6 small, without tops	5
mature, raw	1 about 6 centimeters in diameter	10
mature, cooked	118 milliliters	7
Parsley, raw	15 milliliters chopped	trace
Parsnips, cooked	237 milliliters	23

Vegetables, continued	Measure	Grams Carbohydrate
Peas, green		
cooked	237 milliliters	19
canned	237 milliliters	31
Peppers, green		
raw	2 rings 6 millimeters thick	1
	15 milliliters chopped	trace
cooked	1 medium, about 7 centimeters long, 6 centimeters in diameter	3
Pepper, hot red, without seeds, dried (with ground chili powder and added seasonings)	15 milliliters	8
Potatoes		
baked	1, about 12 centimeters long, 6 centimeters in diameter	21
boiled, peeled after boiling	1, about 6 centimeters in diameter	23
boiled, peeled before boiling	1, about 6 centimeters in diameter	18
chips	10, about 4½ x 6 centimeters	10
French-fried, fresh, cooked in deep fat	10, about 12¾ centimeters long	20
French-fried, frozen, heated, ready-to-serve	10, about 12¾ centimeters long	19

Vegetables, continued	Measure	Grams Carbohydrate
mashed, milk added	237 milliliters	25
mashed, milk and fat added	237 milliliters	24
Pumpkin, canned	118 milliliters	9
Radishes, raw	4 medium	1
Sauerkraut, canned	237 milliliters	9
Spinach, cooked or canned	118 milliliters	3

Squash

summer, cooked	118 milliliters	7
winter, baked	118 milliliters mashed	16

Sweet potatoes

baked in skin	1, about 12¾ centimeters long, 5 centimeters in diameter	36
boiled, peeled after boiling	1, about 12¾ centimeters long, 5 centimeters in diameter	39
candied	one half, about 6 centimeters long	30
canned	118 milliliters mashed	27

Tomatoes

raw	1, about 6 centimeters in diameter	9
cooked or canned	118 milliliters	5
Tomato juice, canned	118 milliliters	5
Turnips, cooked	118 milliliters diced	4
Turnip greens, cooked	237 milliliters	5

Fruits

	Measure	Grams Carbohydrate
Apples, raw	1 medium (about 7 centimeters in diameter)	18
Apple juice, canned	118 milliliters	15
Applesauce		
sweetened	118 milliliters	30
unsweetened	118 milliliters	13
Apricots		
raw	3 (about 26 per kilogram as purchased)	14
canned, heavy syrup pack	237 milliliters halves and syrup	57
dried, cooked, unsweetened	118 milliliters fruit and juice	31
dried, uncooked	20 halves	50
Avocados		
California varieties	284-gram avocado (about 8 centimeters in diameter)	27
Florida varieties	454-gram avocado (about 9¼ centimeters in diameter)	27
Bananas, raw	1	26
Banana flakes	237 milliliters	89
Blackberries, raw	237 milliliters	19
Blueberries, raw	237 milliliters	21
Raspberries		
fresh, red, raw	237 milliliters	17
frozen, red, sweetened	118 milliliters	40

Fruits, continued	**Measure**	**Grams Carbohydrate**
Strawberries		
fresh, raw	237 milliliters	13
frozen, sweetened	118 milliliters sliced	31
Cantaloupe, raw	one half of melon about 12¾ centimeters in diameter	14
Cherries, sour, canned (water packed), pitted	118 milliliters	13
Cranberry sauce, sweetened, canned	59 milliliters	26
Dates, fresh, dried, pitted, cut	118 milliliters	65
Figs, dried	1 large, about 5 x 2½ centimeters	15
Fruit cocktail, canned in heavy syrup	118 milliliters	25
Grapefruit		
raw, white	one half medium (about 9½ centimeters in diameter)	12
raw, pink or red	one half medium (about 9½ centimeters in diameter)	13
canned, syrup pack	237 milliliters	45
Grapefruit juice		
fresh	237 milliliters	23
canned, unsweetened	237 milliliters	24
canned, sweetened	237 milliliters	32
frozen concentrate, diluted, ready-to-serve, unsweetened	237 milliliters	24
made from dehydrated crystals and water	237 milliliters	24

Fruits, continued	Measure	Grams Carbohydrate
Grapes		
American type (Concord, Delaware, Niagara, Scuppernong), slip skin	237 milliliters	15
European type (Malaga, Muscat, Thompson seedless, Flame Tokay), adherent skin	237 milliliters	25
Grape juice		
bottled	118 milliliters	21
frozen concentrate, diluted, ready-to-serve	237 milliliters	33
Grape juice drink, canned	237 milliliters	35
Lemons, raw	1, about 10½ centimeters in diameter	6
Lemon juice, fresh or canned	118 milliliters	10
Lime juice, fresh or canned	118 milliliters	11
Limeade, frozen concentrate, diluted, ready-to-serve	237 milliliters	27
Oranges, raw	1, about 6¾ centimeters in diameter	16
Orange juice		
fresh	118 milliliters	13
canned, unsweetened	118 milliliters	14
frozen concentrate, diluted, ready-to-serve	237 milliliters	29

Fruits, continued	**Measure**	**Grams Carbohydrate**
made from dehydrated crystals and water	237 milliliters	27
Papayas, raw	237 milliliters of 1¼-centimeter cubes	18

Peaches

raw	1 medium (about 6 centimeters in diameter)	10
	118 milliliters sliced	8
canned, water pack	118 milliliters	10
canned, syrup pack	118 milliliters	26
dried, cooked, unsweetened	118 milliliters (5 to 6 halves and liquid)	29
dried, uncooked	237 milliliters	109
frozen, sweetened	118 milliliters	26

Pears

raw	1, about 9 centimeters long, 6 centimeters in diameter	25
canned, syrup pack	118 milliliters	25

Pineapple

raw	237 milliliters diced	19
canned in heavy syrup —crushed, tidbits, or chunks	118 milliliters	25
canned in heavy syrup —sliced	2 small slices or 1 large	24
Pineapple juice, canned	118 milliliters	17

Plums

raw	1, about 5 centimeters in diameter	7

Fruits, continued	Measure	Grams Carbohydrate
canned (syrup pack), with pits	237 milliliters	53
Prunes		
cooked, unsweetened	118 milliliters fruit and liquid	39
uncooked	4	18
Prune juice, canned	237 milliliters	49
Raisins	118 milliliters, packed	64
Rhubarb, cooked, sweetened	118 milliliters	49
Tangerines, raw	1 medium (about 6 centimeters in diameter)	10
Tangerine juice, canned, sweetened	118 milliliters	15
Watermelon, raw	1 wedge about 10 x 20 centimeters	27

Breads

	Measure	Grams Carbohydrate
Boston brown bread	1 slice 7½ x 2 centimeters	22
Cracked wheat bread	1 slice	13
Raisin bread	1 slice	13
Rye bread	1 slice	13
Pumpernickel	1 slice	13
White bread		
soft crumb, regular slice	1 slice	13
soft crumb, thin slice	1 slice	10
firm crumb	1 slice	12

Breads, continued	Measure	Grams Carbohydrate
Whole-wheat bread		
soft crumb	1 slice	14
firm crumb	1 slice	12
French, Italian, or Vienna bread	1 slice	14
Biscuits		
baking powder, home recipe	1, about 5 centimeters in diameter	13
baking powder, from a mix	1, about 5 centimeters in diameter	15
Bagels		
egg bagel	1	28
water bagel	1	30
Crackers		
rye	2, about 5 x 9 centimeters	10
graham	4 small or 2 medium	21
saltine	4, about 5 centimeters square	8
Danish pastry, plain (without fruit or nuts)		
packaged ring	340-gram ring	155
single piece	1, about 11 x 2½ centimeters	30
Doughnuts, cake-type, plain	1, about 8 centimeters in diameter	16
Muffins		
plain	1, about 7½ centimeters in diameter	17

Breads, continued	Measure	Grams Carbohydrate
corn	1, about 6 centimeters in diameter	20

Pancakes

wheat (home recipe or mix)	1, about 10 centimeters in diameter	9
buckwheat (made with buckwheat pancake mix)	1, about 10 centimeters in diameter	6
Pizza (cheese)	13½-centimeter piece (one eighth of 35-centimeter pie)	27
Pretzels, Dutch, twisted	1	12
Pretzels, stick	5 regular (8 centimeters long) or 10 small (5¾ centimeters long)	2

Rolls

hamburger or frankfurter	1 roll (35 per kilogram)	21
hard, round or rectangular	1 roll (20 per kilogram)	30
plain, pan—home recipe	1 roll	20
plain, pan—commercial	1 roll	15
Waffles	1, about 18 centimeters in diameter	28
Bread crumbs, dry	237 milliliters	73

Cereals and Other Grain Products

Bran flakes (40 percent bran)	237 millililters	28

Cereals, continued	Measure	Grams Carbohydrate
Bran flakes with raisins	237 milliliters	40
Corn, puffed, presweet-ened	237 milliliters	27
Corn, shredded	237 milliliters	25
Corn flakes	237 milliliters	21
Corn flakes, sugar-coated	158 milliliters	24
Corn grits, degermed, cooked	237 milliliters	27
Cornmeal, dry	237 milliliters	91
Farina, cooked (quick-cooking)	237 milliliters	22
Macaroni, cooked	178 milliliters	24
Macaroni and cheese		
homemade	118 milliliters	20
canned	118 milliliters	13
Noodles, cooked	237 milliliters	37
Oats, puffed	237 milliliters	19
Oatmeal or rolled oats, cooked	237 milliliters	23
Rice		
regular enriched or unenriched, cooked	237 milliliters	50
"instant," ready-to-serve	237 milliliters	40
Rice, puffed	237 milliliters	13
Spaghetti, cooked	178 milliliters	24
Spaghetti with meat balls		
home recipe	237 milliliters	39
canned	237 milliliters	28

Cereals, continued	Measure	Grams Carbohydrate
Spaghetti in tomato sauce		
with cheese, home recipe	237 milliliters	37
with cheese, canned	237 milliliters	38
Wheat, puffed	237 milliliters	12
Wheat flakes	178 milliliters	18
Wheat, shredded, plain (long, round, or bite-size)	28 grams (1 large biscuit or 118 milliliters bite-size)	20
Wheat flours		
whole wheat	237 milliliters stirred	85
all-purpose	237 milliliters sifted	88
buckwheat, light	237 milliliters	78
self-rising, enriched	237 milliliters	93
cake or pastry	237 milliliters sifted	76

Desserts

	Measure	Grams Carbohydrate
Brownies, with nuts		
homemade	1	10
made from a mix	1	13
Cakes		
angel food cake	6-centimeter piece (one twelfth of 25-centimeter round cake)	32
butter cake, plain, without icing	4½-centimeter piece (one sixteenth of 23-centimeter round cake)	32
	1 cupcake about 7 centimeters in diameter	14

Desserts, continued	Measure	Grams Carbohydrate
buttercake, plain, with chocolate icing	4½-centimeter piece (one sixteenth of 23-centimeter round layer cake)	45
	1 cupcake about 7 centimeters in diameter	21
chocolate, with chocolate icing	4½-centimeter piece (one sixteenth of 23-centimeter round layer cake)	40
	1 cupcake about 7 centimeters in diameter	20
fruitcake, dark	one thirtieth of 20-centimeter loaf	9
gingerbread	1 piece about 7 x 7 x 3½ centimeters	32
pound cake, old-fashioned	1 slice about 9 x 7½ x 1¼ centimeters	14
sponge cake	one twelfth of 25-centimeter round cake	36

Cookies

chocolate chip, home-made	1, about 6 centimeters in diameter	16
chocolate chip, commercial	1	7
fig bars	1 small	11
sandwich, chocolate or vanilla	1, about 4½ centimeters in diameter	7
Custard, baked	237 milliliters	29
Gelatin desserts, plain	118 milliliters	17

Desserts, continued	Measure	Grams Carbohydrate
Ice cream		
regular (about 10 percent fat)	237 milliliters	28
rich (about 16 percent fat)	237 milliliters	27
Ice milk		
hardened	237 milliliters	29
soft serve	237 milliliters	39
Pies		
apple	one eighth of 23-centimeter pie	51
butterscotch	one eighth of 23-centimeter pie	50
Boston cream pie	one twelfth of 20-centimeter round cake	34
cherry	one eighth of 23-centimeter pie	52
custard, plain	one eighth of 23-centimeter pie	30
lemon meringue	one eighth of 23-centimeter pie	45
mince	one eighth of 23-centimeter pie	56
pecan	one eighth of 23-centimeter pie	60
pineapple chiffon	one eighth of 23-centimeter pie	36
pumpkin	one eighth of 23-centimeter pie	32
Piecrust—baked shell made with enriched flour	1 shell	79

Desserts, continued	Measure	Grams Carbohydrate
Piecrust—made from packaged mix	crust for double-crust pie	141
Puddings		
cornstarch, vanilla	237 milliliters	41
cornstarch, chocolate	237 milliliters	67
chocolate, from a mix	118 milliliters	26
tapioca cream	118 milliliters	14
Sherbet	237 milliliters	59

Fats, Oils, and Related Products

	Measure	Grams Carbohydrate
Butter or margarine	15 milliliters	trace
	1 pat 2½ centimeters square, ¾ centimeter thick	trace
Margarine, whipped	15 milliliters	trace
	1 pat 3 centimeters square, ¾ centimeter thick	trace
Cooking fats		
vegetable	15 milliliters	0
lard	15 milliliters	0
Salad or cooking oils	15 milliliters	0
Salad dressings, regular		
blue cheese	15 milliliters	1
French	15 milliliters	3
home-cooked, boiled	15 milliliters	2
mayonnaise	15 milliliters	trace
mayonnaise-type, commercial, plain	15 milliliters	2
thousand island	15 milliliters	3
Salad dressings, low calorie		
French	15 milliliters	trace
mayonnaise-type	15 milliliters	1

Soups

	Measure	Grams Carbohydrate
Bean with pork	237 milliliters	22
Beef noodle	237 milliliters	7
Bouillon, broth, and con- somme	237 milliliters	3
Clam chowder		
Manhattan	237 milliliters	12
New England	237 milliliters	16
Cream of chicken		
with water	237 milliliters	8
with milk	237 milliliters	15
Cream of mushroom		
with water	237 milliliters	10
with milk	237 milliliters	16
Cream of potato		
with water	237 milliliters	12
with milk	237 milliliters	18
Cream of shrimp		
with water	237 milliliters	8
with milk	237 milliliters	15
Dehydrated soups		
chicken noodle	57-gram package	33
onion	42½-gram package	23
tomato vegetable with noodles	71-gram package	45
Minestrone	237 milliliters	14
Oyster stew (frozen)		
with water	237 milliliters	8
with milk	237 milliliters	14
Split pea	237 milliliters	21
Tomato		
with water	237 milliliters	16
with milk	237 milliliters	23

Soups, continued	Measure [2]	Grams Carbohydrate
Vegetable beef	237 milliliters	10
Vegetarian vegetable	237 milliliters	13

Sugars, Sweets, and Related Products

Caramels	28 grams (3 medium caramels)	22
Milk chocolate, sweetened	28-gram bar	16
Chocolate-coated peanuts	28 grams	11
Candy corn	28 grams (20 pieces)	25
Mints	28 grams (3 mints about 4 centimeters in diameter)	25
Fudge, vanilla or chocolate, plain	28 grams	21
Gumdrops	28 grams (2 to 3 large or about 20 small)	25
Hard candy	28 grams (3 to 4 candy balls about 2 centimeters in diameter)	28
Marshmallows	28 grams (4 marsh-mallows—139 per kilogram)	23
Chocolate syrup		
thin type	30 milliliters	24
fudge type	30 milliliters	20
Honey, strained or extracted	15 milliliters	17
Molasses		
cane, light	15 milliliters	13
black strap	15 milliliters	11

Sweets, continued	Measure	Grams Carbohydrate
Syrup, table blends	15 milliliters	15
Jams, preserves	15 milliliters	14
Jellies, marmalades	15 milliliters	13
Sugar		
white, granulated	15 milliliters	11
brown, packed	15 milliliters	13

Beverages

	Measure	Grams Carbohydrate
Alcoholic beverages		
beer, 3.6 percent alcohol by weight	355 milliliters	14
gin, rum, whisky, vodka		
100-proof	44 milliliters	trace
90-proof	44 milliliters	trace
86-proof	44 milliliters	trace
80-proof	44 milliliters	trace
table wines (such as Chablis, claret, Rhine wine, sauterne)	94 milliliters	4
dessert wines (such as muscatel, port, sherry, Tokay)	94 milliliters	8
Carbonated beverages		
carbonated water	355 milliliters	29
ginger ale	355 milliliters	29
cola-type	355 milliliters	37
fruit-flavored soda (10 to 13 percent sugar)	355 milliliters	45
root beer	355 milliliters	45
Tom Collins mix	355 milliliters	45

Beverages, continued	Measure	Grams Carbohydrate
Fruit drinks		
cranberry juice cocktail	118 milliliters	21
grape juice drink	237 milliliters	35
lemonade, frozen concentrate, diluted, ready-to-serve	118 milliliters	14
limeade, frozen concentrate, diluted, ready-to-serve	237 milliliters	27
orange-apricot juice drink	118 milliliters	16
orange-grapefruit juice drink	118 milliliters	13
Fruit juices		
apple juice, canned	118 milliliters	15
grape juice, bottled	118 milliliters	21
grape juice, frozen concentrate, diluted, ready-to-serve	237 milliliters	33
grapefruit juice		
fresh	237 milliliters	23
canned, unsweetened	237 milliliters	24
canned, sweetened	237 milliliters	32
frozen concentrate, diluted, ready-to-serve, unsweetened	237 milliliters	24
made from dehydrated crystals and water	237 milliliters	24
lemon juice, fresh or canned	59 milliliters	5
lime juice, fresh or canned	118 milliliters	11

Beverages, continued	Measure	Grams Carbohydrate
orange juice		
fresh	118 milliliters	13
canned, unsweetened	118 milliliters	14
frozen concentrate, diluted, ready-to-serve	237 milliliters	29
made from dehydrated crystals and water	237 milliliters	27
pineapple juice, canned, unsweetened	118 milliliters	17
prune juice, canned	237 milliliters	49
tangerine juice, canned, sweetened	118 milliliters	15

Milk beverages

cocoa, homemade	237 milliliters	27
chocolate-flavored drink made with skim milk	237 milliliters	27
malted milk	237 milliliters	28

Snacks and Extras

Barbecue sauce	59 milliliters	5
Bouillon cube	1¼-centimeter cube	trace
Olives, green	4 medium, 3 large, or 2 giant	trace
Olives, ripe	3 small or 2 large	trace

Pickles, cucumber

dill	1, about 10 centimeters long, 4½ centimeters in diameter	1

Snacks, continued	Measure	Grams Carbohydrate
sweet	1, about 6 centimeters long, 2 centimeters in diameter	6
fresh	2 slices 4 centimeters in diameter	3
Popcorn, popped (with oil and salt added)	237 milliliters large kernels	5
Potato chips	10, about 4½ x 6 centimeters	10
Pretzels, Dutch, twisted	1	12
Pretzels, stick	5 regular (8 centimeters long) or 10 small 5¾ centimeters long	2
Relish, finely chopped, sweet	15 milliliters	5
Tomato catsup	15 milliliters	4
Tartare sauce	30 milliliters	2
White sauce, medium (made with 237 milliliters milk to 30 milliliters flour and 30 milliliters fat)	118 milliliters	11
Vinegar	15 milliliters	1
Doughnuts, cake-type, plain	1, about 8 centimeters in diameter	16
French fries		
fresh, cooked in deep fat	10, about 5 centimeters long	20
frozen, heated, ready-to-serve	10, about 5 centimeters long	19
Hamburger	57-gram meat patty, with roll	21
Hot dog	1 average, with roll	21

Miscellaneous

	Measure	Grams Carbohydrate
Artichokes, globe or French, boiled	1	15
Bamboo shoots, raw	454 grams or approximately 710 milliliters of 2½-centimeter pieces	24
Caviar, sturgeon, granular or pressed	15 milliliters	1
Limburger cheese	28 grams	1
Chestnuts	10 nuts	31
Chewing gum, candy-coated	1 piece	2
Chop suey, with meat, no noodles, made from home recipe	237 milliliters	13
Chow mein, chicken, no noodles, made from home recipe	237 milliliters	10
Chow mein, canned	237 milliliters	18
Herring		
in tomato sauce	1 herring with 15 milliliters sauce	2
pickled	1 herring	0
smoked, kippered, drained	1 18-centimeter fillet	0
Lobster Newburg	237 milliliters	13
Loquats, raw	10	15
Lychees, raw	10	15
Mangoes, raw	1	39
Pâté de foie gras, canned	15 milliliters	1
Persimmons		
Japanese or kaki	1	33

Miscellaneous, continued	Measure	Grams Carbohydrate
native	1	8
Pigs' feet, pickled	57 grams	0
Pine nuts		
pignolias	28 grams	3
piñon	28 grams	6
Plantains (baking bananas), raw	1	82
Rabbit, domesticated, flesh only, stewed	237 milliliters	0
Sunflower seed kernels, dry	59 milliliters	14
Welsh rarebit	237 milliliters	15

Source Material

"Calories and Weight"
U.S. Department of Agriculture
Information Bulletin No. 364

"Food and Your Weight"
U.S. Department of Agriculture
Home and Garden Bulletin No. 74

"Nutrition Labeling"
U.S. Department of Agriculture
Information Bulletin No. 382

"Nutritive Value of Foods"
U.S. Department of Agriculture
Home and Garden Bulletin No. 72

"Nutritive Value of American Foods in
    Common Units"
U.S. Department of Agriculture
Agriculture Handbook No. 456